How God Found Me on the Streets of Baghdad

S. JOSEPH KIDDER

Pacific Press®
Publishing Association

Nampa, Idaho | Oshawa, Ontario, Canada
www.pacificpress.com

Cover design by Gerald Lee Monks
Cover design resources from 165764649 | jameslee1 / 895492664 | Greens87
Inside design by Kristin Hansen-Mellish

The author assumes full responsibility for the accuracy of all facts and quotations as cited in this book.

Additional copies of this book can be purchased by calling toll-free 1-800-765-6955 or by visiting http://www.AdventistBookCenter.com.

ISBN 978-0-8163-6384-1

January 2018

Dedication

I want to dedicate this book to the Seventh-day Adventist church in Baghdad, Iraq, where I found Jesus, who changed my life. I pray God will bless you, empower you, and sustain you in the midst of enormous challenges.

Also by S. Joseph Kidder

Majesty: Experiencing Authentic Worship

The Big Four: Secrets to a Thriving Church Family

Youth Speaks: The Church Listens

Moving Your Church: Become a Spirit-Led Community

Contents

Acknowledgements

I would like to acknowledge Katelyn Weyant, who worked with me on Mondays and Wednesdays and often sacrificed Fridays and Sundays to read this book. You gave great insight to improve and make this book better. You have been a blessing.

Divine Appointments

God's Miraculous Encounters That Changed My Life

"Now this is eternal life: that they know you,
the only true God, and Jesus Christ, whom you have sent."
—John 17:3

I found Jesus on the streets of Bagdad, Iraq. However, I never thought that a random walk with my cousin one sultry Friday afternoon would turn out to be the most significant event in my life. That walk was not random; it was a divine appointment from God. It taught me that the Lord is guiding me, and He has a great plan for my life.

What I encountered during that walk led me to know Jesus and eventually give my heart to Him. My faith and commitment to Jesus Christ and my determination to stand firm for Him caused me to fail two years of schooling because I refused to take the exams on the Sabbath. I also lost a scholarship that covered four years of education and was kicked out of university.

One day during the summer of 1975, after all of these events had occurred, there was a gathering at my home with about one hundred upset relatives. They were disappointed with my newfound faith that led me to lose the education they had hoped for me. I was spit upon, humiliated, beaten almost to death, and thrown out on the street. However, three decades after that event, I am able to see that through this experience of loss, a beating, and humiliation came the greatest blessing of my life. In fact, I am alive today because of that experience.

My testimony shows that when we surrender everything to God and are totally committed to Him, we might face persecution and difficulties, but eventually, He will make all things to work together for our good (Romans 8:28). I encountered this to the fullest.

After forty years of knowing and walking with Jesus, I know, beyond any shadow of a doubt, the meaning of the words in Jeremiah 29:11: "'I know the plans I have for you,' declares the Lord, . . . 'plans to give you hope and a future.'" These words are not just sentimental words that God gave us; rather, they are His ideal purpose for our lives. God is in the business of leading His people. He knows everything about us—where we sit down, our thoughts, and where we go (Psalm 139:1–3). He knows where we live and what we do for a living (Revelation 2:13). He knows the desire of our hearts and even the number of hairs on our heads (Matthew 10:30).

I am amazed that God takes all the mosaics of our lives—all the little and big events, all the problems and challenges—and puts them together in such a way that when we look back, it makes perfect sense. We will see how God has intervened in our lives and fit the pieces together flawlessly. As you look back at your past, through the eyes of faith, you will see that behind every event in your life, God is working everything out for good. Our role is to seek the Lord with all of our heart, mind, and soul. If we do that, we will find Him, and He will pour out His abundant blessings upon us (see Deuteronomy 4:29–31).

Jesus revealed Himself, His power, and His grace to me through many experiences and relationships. He spoke in many different ways as His providence guided me.

Learning about and choosing to follow Jesus was the best thing that ever happened to me. It changed the trajectory of my life. I found in Him a wonderful Friend, loving Savior, and great Lord. My prayer is that you will experience the same.

As you read my story, reflect on how God has led in your life as you see how He has led in mine. My prayer is that, at the end, you will stand in awe and say, "What a Great God we have."

This is a story about the amazing love of God and the importance of surrendering to Him. It is a story about the incredible power of God released through prayer. This is the testimony of God's redemption of one man from Nineveh.

Finding God in Baghdad

God's Purpose and Guidance in My Life

*This is good, and pleases God our Savior, who wants all people to
be saved and to come to knowledge of the truth.*
—1 Timothy 2:3, 4

I come from Mosul—the biblical city of Nineveh—which is located in northern Iraq. The name Nineveh lives on since the modern city and the ruins of the ancient city are called the District of Nineveh, and the region is called the state of Nineveh.

About 2,760 years ago, God sent Jonah the prophet to Nineveh. He led the Assyrians who lived there to worship the one true God. At some point in history, Nineveh returned to their old way of worshiping idols, but God never forgot about Nineveh. Hundreds of years after their original conversion, tradition has it that Thomas went east and was able to convert many people in Iraq, Syria, Lebanon, and India to Christianity—including Nineveh. Over time, because of persecution and discrimination, the vast majority of Christians in that region have migrated to the West. Others have been killed, and some have converted to Islam.

Jonah continues to be an integral part of Mosul. When I was growing up, everyone in the state of Nineveh was urged to participate in the fast of Jonah at least once in their life by not eating or drinking anything for three days and three nights. At the heart of Mosul's downtown area was the grave of Jonah. (Jonah's grave was destroyed by ISIS in July of 2014.)[1] All the major roads led to his grave or went around it, reminding all the people to repent and turn to the mighty God who can give them forgiveness and a new life.

The walk that changed my life

My father was a businessman who had moved his business from Nineveh to Baghdad for better opportunities. We lived in a suburb outside the city called New Baghdad.

I was born in a nominal Christian home. My parents belonged to the Christian Orthodox Church, which is very similar to the Catholic Church. I do not recall my father ever going to church, not even for Christmas or Easter. My mother showed a little more interest in God. She went to church a few times a year. I received hardly any biblical instruction, and I knew very little about the nature of my faith. I lived a very happy and contented life, but things started to change one boring afternoon.

My dream as a teenager was to be a professional soccer player. My idol in life was Pelé, the Brazilian soccer legend from the 1970s. Millions of young boys from all over the world wanted to be like him. Obviously I was not the one who took his place. Nevertheless, my passion for soccer drove me to practice almost daily.

One Friday afternoon in the summer of 1971, I invited my cousin Basher to come to my house and spend the afternoon playing backgammon and practicing soccer. My cousin was a very strange fellow. He was, apparently, the only person in Iraq who did not appreciate soccer, nor like to play it. After about twenty minutes of practicing, he said he was done and wanted to go for a walk. By accident, or better yet, by divine providence, our walk brought us to the Adventist church.

There was a small sign (about six by five inches) advertising a movie about the life of Jesus Christ and inviting people to go in and watch it. If the sign had been any larger, the pastor would have been arrested and put in jail. In Iraq, any form of evangelism, public or personal, is against the law and is forbidden. But the pastor was innovative and took the risk to experiment with this form of evangelism, hoping and praying someone would see the ad and go in to watch the movie. My cousin saw the ad, looked at me, and said, "We don't have any-thing to do. Let's go in and watch the movie. We might learn something new."

We went in and saw Jesus on the screen. I saw Him performing miracles, teaching the crowds, and dying for our sins. As I watched, I was struck by how loving and kind Jesus was and also by the power that raised Him from the dead. I thought, *Here's Somebody who loved me so much that He died for me!* I was moved and amazed, and I fell in love with Him.

After the movie, Pastor Hillal Doss gave a devotional message about watchfulness. He said, "Christ took His disciples to Gethsemane to stay up and pray with Him, but they slept [Matthew 26:40]. What about us? Are we awake with Jesus, or are we sleeping?"

Getting to know Jesus

The movie and message touched my heart so much that I went to the pastor and asked him to teach me more about Jesus—the Bible study lasted for over four months. During that time, he taught me about the major stories of the Old Testament, such as Creation, the Fall, the Flood, the Exodus, the Babylonian captivity, and the Israelites' deliverance from captivity, as well as the prophecies. Then we moved into the New Testament—the birth of Jesus, His life, the miracles He performed, His death and resurrection, the acts of His apostles, and His second coming.

My love and appreciation for Jesus deepened during that time as I learned more and more about Him and His love and plan for my life. For me, these Bible studies were life-changing. I learned so much, and I got a broader perspective on life. I wanted to spend time learning about the God who loved me so much that gave His Son to die on the cross for me. I was very eager to go to church every week on Tuesday after I finished school for another Bible study.

As we fall in love with someone, we intentionally focus on that relationship and desire to spend more time with that person. In the same way, our love for Jesus will deepen as we intentionally spend time with Him in prayer and Bible study.

In 1 Chronicles, King David advised the leaders of Israel to set their hearts and souls to seek the Lord, their God (1 Chronicles 22:19). From the first time I met Jesus on the screen, I chose to seek Him. My heart was thrilled with His grace. So I began a lifelong pursuit of God through Bible study, prayer, and worship.

If we desire intimacy with Him, it is necessary for us to approach the spiritual disciplines purposefully. I learned before opening Scripture to ask the Lord what He wants to say to me. Pray to understand His ways—He loves answering that request. Enter His presence with the intention of knowing His will, living His truth, and feeling His grace and presence.

As I studied the Bible with the pastor, I felt what Isaiah said to his Lord and God, Yahweh, "My soul yearns for you in the night; in the morning my spirit longs for you" (Isaiah 26:9). I was determined to seek the Lord with all my heart, mind, and soul. I did this even when I did not feel like putting the time into my relationship with Christ. Sometimes the Bible studies were amazing, and the Spirit of God touched me deeply. Sometimes they fell flat. If you fall in love with Christ, you are a Christian and are born of the Spirit. Christianity is not a religion. It's a relationship with God.

The more you come to know Him, the more He sets your heart on fire with love for others and Himself. His love for us is infinite, and He proved it by dying for us on the cross. Once you come to see His true nature and how much He cares for all of us, you can't help but begin to feel the same.

The Adventist pastor said something that deeply impacted me, "If you were the only person that God ever created, He would have sent His Son to die for you. Think about that for a bit. You are one out of 3.7 billion people on planet Earth, yet God valued your life by the value of the life of His Son, whom He sent to die for you. When you experience this kind of love, you will want to have a lifelong journey to know the heart of God."

Then he asked me, "Who do you love here on earth? Why do you love them?" He continued by saying, "I really love my mom and dad with all of my heart, and I know about them because of that love. Knowing all these things about them, and how much they care for me, drives me to love them even more. It is the same thing with Jesus. The more we know Him, the more we will love Him."

In the struggles of life, we can become distracted and not really take the time to just be with our Lord. Visit Christ in His Word. That would be a great place to start. We are all on a journey to know the heart of God. Think about who Jesus is and how important His friendship is to you. Pray and receive His presence and grace. Then think of Him dying on the cross for you. He died so that you might live. Should we not be head over heels in love with Him?

In John 15:15, Jesus says, "I no longer call you servants, because a servant does not know his master's business. Instead, I have called you friends, for everything that I learned from my Father I have made known to you."

Jesus will come to you with words of healing or words of comfort, and perhaps as the relationship deepens, words of reproof and correction. There will also come a time for Him to clean up the well of our lives and hearts, creating positive and lasting changes in us.

My appeal to you is to fall in love with Jesus. He will open rivers of living water inside of you.

A time of testing

I loved everything I learned about Jesus. Then, one day, I went to church to have another Bible study, but we didn't have one. The pastor looked at me and said, "You have been coming here for several months to learn about Jesus. It's time for you to accept Jesus into your heart." That was very hard because I grew up in a culture where if you changed your faith from that of your parents', they killed you. If society and family didn't kill you, they ostracized you, shunned you, and made your life miserable. If you left the comfort and security of your parents' faith and home, you lost your support system. I didn't want any of that to happen to me, so I thought seriously about quitting the Bible study.[2]

Before I tell you about the decision I made, let me tell you about my first Bible.

---

1. Dana Ford and Mohammed Tawfeeq, "Extremists Destroy Jonah's Tomb, Officials Say," CNN, July 25, 2014, http://www.cnn.com/2014/07/24/world/iraq-violence/.

2. There is only one type of conversion allowed in the Middle East by law and tradition—from Christianity to Islam. Very few Christians become Muslim, and the few Muslims who become Christians have to leave the country in order to save their lives. Changing denominations in the Christian community is only acceptable from Orthodox to Catholic, or vice versa. The Orthodox and Catholic Church communities frown upon members converting to Protestantism—particularly to Seventh-day Adventism.

My First Bible

God's Word Transformed My Life

Your word is a lamp for my feet,
a light on my path.

—Psalm 119:105

After my first time going to the Adventist church on Friday night to watch the movie about the life of Christ, I started to study the Bible with Pastor Hillal Doss on Tuesday afternoons. A few weeks later, I started to go to Sabbath School and, occasionally, the worship service. At that time, I was in middle school. Because of the lack of school buildings in Iraq, they divided the students into two groups. One group attended school on Sabbath mornings from 8:00 A.M. to noon. Then the second group attended from 1:00 P.M. to 5:00 P.M. They rotated the students every month. When my time to go to school was in the afternoon, I went to the Adventist church in the morning.

I enjoyed the worship service—studying the Bible, singing, and fellowship. Some young people invited me to go to the youth department and included me in every social activity. While there, I met Muneer and Selma, who became close friends. This couple mentored me. They taught me to pray, read the Bible, and discern God's will. God used them to minister to me and teach me many things. I was blessed to have them disciple me.

This was in direct contrast to the Orthodox church that I attended from time to time with my mother, where the emphasis was on the liturgy. The few times I went to the Orthodox church with my mother, I did not get anything out of it. The language was Neo-Aramaic, and I spoke Arabic. There was little emphasis on reading the Bible. I was very hungry to know God and His will, and that is what made me feel at home at the Adventist church.

One Sabbath, Pastor Doss of the Adventist church in Bagdad preached about the Bible. His sermon left a strong impression, and it led me to work for six months to purchase my first Bible.

The Word of God endures forever

Pastor Doss had a few points in his sermon:

1. *The Bible is the Word of God.* "All Scripture is God-breathed and is useful for teaching, rebuking, correcting and training in righteousness, so that the servant of God may be thoroughly equipped for every good work" (2 Timothy 3:16, 17).

As we breathe our words, so God breathes the words of Scripture. They are His thoughts expressed in words. "Above all, you must understand that no prophecy of Scripture came about by the prophet's own interpretation of things. For prophecy never had its origin in the human will, but prophets, though human, spoke from God as they were carried along by the Holy Spirit" (2 Peter 1:20, 21). All of our teaching should be based upon Scripture, which will equip men and women of God to do every good work.

2. *The Bible can change your life.* "For the word of God is alive and active. Sharper than any double-edged sword, it penetrates even to dividing soul and spirit, joints and marrow; it judges the thoughts and attitudes of the heart" (Hebrews 4:12). Only God can change hearts and set addicts free, allow abusers and narcissistic people to become men and women of God. "If you abide in My word, you are My disciples indeed. And you shall know the truth, and the truth shall make you free" (John 8:31, 32, NKJV).

3. *The Bible will stand forever.* "But the word of the Lord endures forever. And this is the word that was preached to you" (1 Peter 1:25).

The Bible has been under attack for centuries—from everything you can imagine, including the government, other religions, and atheism. Yet the Bible is still the most read, most published, and most translated book in the world. Most important, it's still changing the lives of those who apply what it teaches.

One of the reasons I believe the Bible is God's Word is that it has flourished in spite of unrelenting attacks during the past two thousand years. Jesus said in Matthew 24:35, "Heaven and earth will pass away, but my words will never pass away." The only item on the planet that will last is the Word of God because truth is eternal. Everything else will burn up.

The Bible always survives—and it always will. You can depend on that. "The grass withers and the flowers fall, but the word of our God endures forever" (Isaiah 40:8).

Jesus, the Light of the World

When I heard this sermon, my heart was touched, and I was determined to get my own Bible. I wanted to read it for myself and have Jesus change me as He had changed Peter, Paul, John, and others. However, getting my first Bible turned out to be a challenging endeavor.

In Bagdad, it was difficult to obtain a Bible. It cost about one hundred dollars, and sometimes it took up to a year to get one. I was about sixteen when I decided to own my own Bible. I did not want to ask the church to give me one because I didn't want to cost them money. I wanted to work for my own Bible so that it would be special to me. I worked hard for my dad and earned one hundred dollars and gave it to the government, registering my name to get a Bible. After eight months, I got a notice that my Bible was ready to pick up. After school one day, I went to pick it up. I was so excited that I immediately went home, hoping to read it.

My mother, who was a very loving woman, was also very strict when it came to homework. We couldn't do anything—no television, no sports, no playing outside—unless our homework was done first. She would help us and make sure we did it correctly. I got home around 4:00 P.M. after picking up my Bible and worked on my homework until 10:00 P.M. My mom inspected my work and then told my brother and me it was time for bed. I really wanted to read my Bible, so after my brother had fallen asleep, I went to the kitchen and got a flashlight. I got back into bed with my Bible, pulled the covers over my head, and turned on the flashlight. Someone had told me to start reading in the book of John. I fumbled my way through and found it. I just happened to land on John 8:12, which reads, "When Jesus spoke again to the people, he said, 'I am the light of the world. Whoever follows me will never walk in darkness, but will have the light of life.'" When I read these words, I was filled with so much joy and excitement that my heart started beating really fast. My eyes were filled with sparkle, and I determined in my heart that Jesus would be the light of my life!

As I was immersed in reading, I didn't notice that my mom had gone to the kitchen to prepare the meals for the next day. On her way back to her bedroom, she decided to check on us. When she opened our door, she saw the beam of light shining through the blanket. She was terrified, wondering what her son was reading. She pulled back the blanket, and to her surprise, she found me reading my Bible. She let out a huge sigh of relief and said, "You have twenty minutes to read, then go to sleep."

That was my first personal encounter with the Bible, and I fell in love with the Word of God. After this, I read it consistently and with passion, even going to the pastor of the Adventist church for pointers on how to read it. He told me to start with the New Testament, and when I was finished, go to the Old Testament. I got my Bible sometime in March and had finished reading it by November. I looked forward to reading it every day! I learned all of the stories of the life and teachings of Jesus, the stories of Acts, the teachings of the apostle Paul, and all the stories of the Old Testament. The result was that I fell in love more deeply and passionately with my Lord and Savior, Jesus Christ.

Meeting God in His Word

Since that time, I have cherished the Word of God. I study it every day. I have become closer to Christ, and it has changed my life.

I learned when it comes to reading the Bible to prepare my heart. I talk to God about things I may need to confess, and enter my study time peacefully and without anything that may block me from receiving His revelation and will for my life.

I make the time to study because there is power in it to change my life and allow me to become the person God wants me to be. Once you take the time to read the Bible, you'll experience peace, joy, and wisdom every day of your life!

Don't just study God's Word for the sake of studying. Be sure to put the Word into practice in your life. Jesus said in Luke 11:28, "But even more blessed are all who hear the word of God and put it into practice" (NLT). When God speaks to you through His Word, be sure to apply those nuggets to your day-to-day life.

When I study the Bible, it's not just to gain knowledge but also to learn more about God and to apply His truths to my life. The Bible testifies to itself as being a living book. Therefore, we don't merely fill our minds with the facts and principles of Scripture. That would be lifeless. Instead, we listen to what God is saying about how to apply His Word.

When I study the Bible, I look closely at the text. Sometimes it helps to compare different translations or look up words in a Bible dictionary. It is very useful to compare it with other similar verses in the Bible and get the bigger picture.

I ask myself:

- What is the main truth of this passage?
- What is a key verse? Consider memorizing it.
- Who are the main characters?
- Is there any example to follow or to avoid?
- Is there a promise for me to claim?

One of the first Scripture passages I memorized was Philippians 4:6, 7: "Be anxious for nothing, but in everything by prayer and supplication with thanksgiving let your requests be made known to God. And the peace of God, which surpasses all comprehension, shall guard your hearts and your minds in Christ Jesus" (NASB). It remains one of my favorite verses to this day.

In the middle of my persecution, this was a great comfort for me. Despite my circumstances, God gave me peace and assured me that He was in charge of my life.

As I worked to memorize the words, dwelling on them, I also began to surrender my anxious thoughts, confirming firsthand that the peace of God really does surpass understanding. That is the way God transforms us. By dwelling on the text, God removed my anxiety. He does the same thing with every text we read in the Scripture.

Ultimately, we read the Bible for the purpose of knowing God. "You will seek and find me when you seek me with all your heart" (Jeremiah 29:13; see Deuteronomy 4:29). "When I am lifted up from the earth, I will draw everyone to myself" (John 12:32, NLT).

With Bible study, if we show up, God will meet us in His Word.

Wrestling With the Lord

God's Persistent Pursuit of Me

For our struggle is not against flesh and blood,
but against the rulers, against the authorities,
against the powers of this dark world and against
the spiritual forces of evil in the heavenly realms.

—Ephesians 6:12

After about four months of studying the Bible with Pastor Hillal Doss and learning more and more about Jesus and the plan of salvation, I was confronted with accepting Jesus as my Lord and Savior. That was hard for me because of the persecution I knew I would face. I did not want any harm to come to me, so I decided to quit the Bible study and go back to my normal life. But the Lord never gave up on me. He kept pursuing me. Every day, I felt the nudging of the Holy Spirit to go back again and study the Bible.

In my struggle to accept Jesus and be fully committed to Him in every aspect of my life, I was caught between the forces of good and evil. The devil and the world seemed enticing, but I felt the gentle push of the Holy Spirit to go back to the Bible study every day. Praise God that He never gives up on us. He cares so much that He keeps pursuing us. Like David, I could say, "Where can I go from your Spirit? Where can I flee from your presence? If I go up to the heavens, you are there; if I make my bed in the depths, you are there" (Psalm 139:7, 8).

Finally I surrendered to the Holy Spirit, and I went to the pastor for another Bible study. This time, we had a Bible study on the Ten Commandments. I did not have any problem with the Ten Commandments, except for the fourth one about the Sabbath. The Bible study was very simple. Pastor Doss said, "God kept it. Jesus kept it. The disciples kept it. We are going to keep it in heaven. Why don't we keep it now?" That made perfect sense to me. Plus, in Arabic, the language I grew up in, we don't have names for the days of the week. Sunday is called the "First Day." Monday is called the "Second Day." The only one that does have a name in Arabic is the seventh day, called the "Sabbath." Everybody knew it was a day of rest. My problem was that the day off in Iraq was and is Friday, and everybody is required to go to school and to work on the Sabbath. So I said to myself, *I will never have a future in Iraq. I will never be able to finish my schooling. I will never be able to find a job. If the Sabbath is really the Lord's Day, then I'll have to change religions and become a Seventh-day Adventist. But if I change my faith, I'll become a source of shame for my family, and they'll most likely disown me.*

Second opinion

I was very disturbed, so I left the Adventist pastor and said to myself, *I need a second opinion.* A few days later, I went and visited with a Greek Orthodox priest. After I explained to him my dilemma, he lifted up the Bible and said, "If you go by the Bible, you need to keep the seventh-day Sabbath holy." I was very disappointed in what he said to me.

A few weeks later, I went and visited with a Catholic priest. He said to me, "We changed the day."

A few days after that, I went to visit with the pastor of the largest Protestant denomination of that time, the Presbyterians. Unbeknownst to me, the Adventist pastor had befriended the Presbyterian pastor. For Christmas, he gave him a book, *The Great Controversy.* He read the book, and when I met with him, he said to me, "I have been struggling with this issue, and I have decided that we really need to keep the seventh-day Sabbath holy." I said to him, "This is not what I wanted to hear from you." I left him and decided not to visit with any other pastor because they all told me the same thing!

Later on, this Presbyterian pastor became a Seventh-day Adventist, and

I witnessed his baptism. The Lord had been working on his heart, and he responded positively. At the time of his baptism, he said he appreciated that the Adventist pastor took the time to develop a relationship with him. He went on to say that he had discovered the truth as a result of reading the book *The Great Controversy*. This book was life-changing for him.

Once I became convinced that, according to the Bible, Saturday was the Lord's Day, the Sabbath, I was faced with the deeper struggle, the struggle to obey God and keep His day holy.

For the next two years, I thought of the problems I would face if I took my stand to keep the Sabbath day holy and join the Adventist Church. I thought of how I would lose my family and my friends if I started observing the Sabbath and practicing my new faith.

Families in the Middle East are very close. Changing my faith would be denying my family and going against them, resulting in disownment. I knew I would become a source of shame.

There were other problems I had to consider. In Iraq, every male is required to serve for two years in the army after high school or college. I was afraid of facing problems dealing with Sabbath keeping and bearing arms. I was also worried about fighting in a war, since wars start in the Middle East anytime, anywhere.

What difference does it make?

When I thought about these challenges, I started to rationalize and say to myself, *What difference does it make to keep the Sabbath on Saturday? Every day is the Sabbath day, you just choose one day and the Lord will understand.* But the Holy Spirit was reminding me that we are in the mess of sin today because two people said, "What difference does it make if you eat from this tree or that tree? They are all trees." It is not about the tree. It is not about the day. It is about our love, loyalty, and allegiance to Jesus Christ. Obedience to the Lord is extremely important.

The Holy Spirit also reminded me that God blessed and kept the seventh day. Therefore, God wants us to do the same. It was important for God to keep it. Therefore, it must be important for us.

I was thinking, *Is it possible that all those people who do not keep the Sabbath day holy are wrong? How about all of these other churches? Could 1.2 billion Christians be mistaken?*

Something better

It was at that time that I graduated from high school. Iraq had a system where if you graduated with a certain GPA, you were eligible to take another exam called the Baccalaureate Exam. If you scored in the ninetieth percentile or higher, you were allowed to go to any college of your choice free for four years; but if you scored in the seventieth percentile or lower, you were sent straight to the army. I studied hard and did well on the exam. I received a scholarship to the School of Engineering, which entitled me to four years of free college education.

This scholarship provided an excuse for me to avoid making my decision for Christ. During my first year at the university, I hardly ever attended church or read the Bible. I prayed from time to time over exams and papers or a difficult situation in life. To some degree, I felt I had already arrived and was not in need of anything. Yet on the other hand, I often felt as though there was something better in life than material possessions. The Holy Spirit kept nudging me to make a decision for Christ, and occasionally, I would seriously consider it.

Education was very important in Iraq, and it was my opportunity to live what I thought would be a happy, wonderful life. During my first year at the university, I struggled tremendously, caught between Christ on one side and the world on the other. The world seemed too good to leave, but the Holy Spirit reminded me about Jesus—He was too good to ignore. Jesus was worth everything. I knew that men and women had left everything—family, friends, relatives, and jobs—to follow Him. They lived and died for Him.

The Orthodox priest's sermon

At the university in Baghdad where I attended, there was a tradition. All of the exams came on one day, the seventh-day Sabbath. The day started at 9:00 A.M. and went until 6:00 P.M. The Sunday before my final exams, something unusual happened. My mother was a casual Christian, but she was very consistent in her church attendance. She went to the Orthodox church twice a year, Christmas and Easter. On that Sunday, there was a celebration of the ascension of Jesus into heaven at her church, and she wanted to go. When you are not in the habit of going to church every week, it's hard to go, so she came to me and begged me to go to church with her. I came up with every excuse I could come up with, but finally I gave in. I do not know if it was to please her or get her off my back, but I said, "Fine, Mom. I will go to church with you."

My mother belonged to a very large church with several thousand members, but on a regular Sunday there would be less than one hundred elderly women. However, on Christmas and Easter, thousands would come for multiple services throughout the day. My mom and I went to the church, and the place was completely full, so we sat in the back. After one hour of liturgy, the pastor began preaching.

The Orthodox priest stood up in front of the large crowd gathered to celebrate Jesus' ascension into heaven and said, "My heart is troubled. Something happened to me last night that has never happened to me before. The Lord woke me up in the middle of the night and gave me another message for you. The new message is on martyrdom." For someone who had not been to church in a while, the last subject I wanted to hear about was death. I wanted to listen to topics about faith, hope, or positive thinking, but certainly not death. Despite my disappointment, that sermon was the defining moment in my life. In fact, that sermon changed my life.

The Orthodox priest opened the Scriptures and read from Matthew 19:27–29:

> Peter answered him, "We have left everything to follow you! What then will there be for us?" Jesus said to them, "Truly I tell you, at the renewal of all things, when the Son of Man sits on his glorious throne, you who have followed me will also sit on twelve thrones, judging the twelve tribes of Israel. And everyone who has left houses or brothers or sisters or father or mother or wife or children or fields for my sake will receive a hundred times as much and will inherit eternal life."

The Orthodox priest started his sermon talking about the sacrifice Jesus made on our behalf at the cross. He spoke of how the King of the whole universe stepped down and became a man that lived, suffered, and died for our sake. The question he asked was shouldn't we do the same? God is calling us to follow the example of Jesus, to forsake all and follow Him.

He continued preaching very passionately about the disciples, the apostles, and the early Christians, who, for the sake of Jesus, left their homes, possessions, and families to follow Him. Jesus was everything to them, and for His glory, they gave their lives and suffered hardship and endured persecution. If Jesus gave up everything for us, even His life, shouldn't we desire to do the same? If the disciples gave their lives to Him, shouldn't we follow their example and give up everything in simple trust and follow Jesus?

I was sitting in church with thousands of other people, and I felt God's presence in such a way that I never felt before. I felt that He was inside of me and all around me. I felt like heaven was opened up, and I saw Jesus sitting on the throne loving me. To paraphrase the words of John Wesley, "My heart was strangely warmed by the grace of God." I started to cry, and I determined in my heart that I would follow Jesus no matter what.

I was touched by the Holy Spirit, who spoke to me, telling me that following Jesus was worth it. There will be persecution and there will be problems, but Jesus with His love will always be with us. At that moment, God's peace entered my heart, and I decided to follow Him all the way. At the end of the worship service, I turned to my mother and said to her, "Go home, and I will see you there later."

As I was leaving the Orthodox church, I started to think about all of the challenges that I would face if I became an Adventist. Every imaginable negative scenario came to my mind. I would not only lose my family, but I also might lose my schooling and scholarship. Chances were good that I would never have a job in the future. I might even lose my life.

I left the Orthodox church and started roaming the streets of Baghdad, thinking about what would happen to me if I accepted Jesus.

Deliverance in the Fire

God's Reign in My Life

Blessed is the one who perseveres under trial because,
having stood the test, that person will receive the crown of life that
the Lord has promised to those who love him.

—James 1:12

The decision to follow Jesus is not always easy to make. It is full of trials, temptations, and difficulties. Throughout the Bible, there are people who, for the sake of Christ, left homes and family to endure hardship and even death. But somehow, in the end, God turned their defeat into victory and their trial into triumph. This is what God promised in James 1:12, and we know that He is always faithful to His promises.

I heard the sermon by the Greek Orthodox priest about how Jesus gave His life for us, and we should do the same for Him. I listened to him describe how the disciples left their homes, moms and dads, and brothers and sisters to follow Jesus. They are our examples. We need to do the same. I felt God's presence, and I had determined in my heart that I would follow Jesus no matter what.

When the worship service was over, I left in a different direction than my mom and started walking on the streets of Baghdad, full of fear of what would happen to me if I followed Jesus. I thought of the persecution I would face from my family, the loss I would incur at the university, and what others would think of me.

Finally, five hours later, I ended up at the home of the Seventh-day Adventist pastor. I told Pastor Doss about the sermon I heard in the Orthodox church and my decision. I also confessed my fears to him. He said, "Let me tell you a story that took place about sixty miles from my home in Baghdad."

Filled with boldness

Pastor Doss told me the story of Shadrach, Meshach, and Abednego, the three friends who were commanded to bow to the image of the Babylonian king but refused. Furious, the king asked the three friends if it was true that they would not worship his image nor serve his gods. He gave them a second chance to fall down and worship the image when they heard the music, and if they did not, he threatened to throw them into the blazing furnace, saying, "Then what god will be able to rescue you from my hand?" (Daniel 3:15).

Shadrach, Meshach, and Abednego, filled with boldness, replied to him: "King Nebuchadnezzar, we do not need to defend ourselves before you in this matter. If we are thrown into the blazing furnace, the God we serve is able to deliver us from it, and he will deliver us from Your Majesty's hand. But even if he does not, we want you to know, Your Majesty, that we will not serve your gods or worship the image of gold you have set up" (Daniel 3:16–18).

After reading the text, the pastor shared with me insights that I will remember for the rest of my life. He said, "Those three friends most likely prayed that God would deliver them *from* the fire, but God through His infinite wisdom decided to deliver them *in* the fire. Think about it. Because God decided to deliver them in the fire, they had the greatest worship experience of their lives. Right there in the fire, Jesus showed up, and they worshiped Him and walked with Him. The Babylonian king, Nebuchadnezzar, leaped to his feet in amazement and said, 'I see four men loose, walking in the midst of the fire; and they are not hurt, and the form of the fourth is like the Son of God' [Daniel 3:25]. The king saw the three friends in the fire walking with Jesus and worshiping Him."

Pastor Doss said to me, "The minds of the three friends were made up to worship God. For them, it was a matter of principle not to worship false gods, whatever might be the consequences. Their attention was fixed on what was right, not on what would be the result. They had no concern about what would follow. True faith is determined to do what is right and not to do wrong—whatever the consequences. It matters not what follows—wealth or poverty, honor or shame, good report or evil report, life or death—the mind is firmly fixed on Jesus and on doing right."

Our hope in the words of Jesus

When it comes to persecution, trials, or difficulties, our hope is in the words of Jesus:

"Blessed are those who are persecuted for righteousness' sake, for theirs is the kingdom of heaven. Blessed are you when they revile and persecute you, and say all kinds of evil against you falsely for My sake. Rejoice and be exceedingly glad, for great is your reward in heaven, for so they persecuted the prophets who were before you" (Matthew 5:10–12, NKJV).

Pastor Doss continued, "This is 'the religion of commitment.' These three friends were young. They had few opportunities for instruction in the nature of their faith. They were captives in a distant land. These friends stood before the absolute monarch, with no powerful people to support them, and with a horrid death threatening them. When we consider the circumstances of those who made this reply, we may well admire the grace of God who could so amply furnish them with boldness and grace for such a trial. He gave them a faith so strong, which enabled them to take a stand so noble and so brave."

Those Hebrew friends experienced the power of God in an awesome way. God saved them from the fiery furnace. Like the psalmist, they could say,

The Lord is my light and my salvation—
    whom shall I fear?
The Lord is the stronghold of my life—
    of whom shall I be afraid?

When the wicked advance against me
    to devour me,
it is my enemies and my foes
    who will stumble and fall.
Though an army besiege me,
    my heart will not fear;

though war break out against me,
even then I will be confident (Psalm 27:1–3).

When the time came to stand faithful to God, God strengthened them by His grace. "After you have suffered for a little while, the God of all grace, who called you to His eternal glory in Christ, will Himself perfect, confirm, strengthen and establish you" (1 Peter 5:10, NASB).

Then the pastor said, "Because God decided to deliver them in the fire, they experienced the power of God." The Bible tells us that the people who threw them into the fire died from the intensity of the heat, but nothing happened to the young men, not even the smell of smoke was on their clothes. The Babylonian officials and the king's counselors gathered together and saw that the fire had no power over Shadrach, Meshach, and Abednego. Not even the hair on their heads was scorched, nor their garments affected (Daniel 3:21, 27).

The promise of Isaiah 43:1, 2 was indeed fulfilled in their lives:

But now, this is what the LORD says—
he who created you, Jacob,
he who formed you, Israel:
"Do not fear, for I have redeemed you;
I have summoned you by name; you are mine.
When you pass through the waters,
I will be with you;
and when you pass through the rivers,
they will not sweep over you.
When you walk through the fire,
you will not be burned;
the flames will not set you ablaze."

When people are faithful to God, He will walk through the fire with them.

The pastor continued, "Because God decided to deliver them in the fire, they became a witness and an inspiration to people of that time and Christians throughout all the ages." Even King Nebuchadnezzar acknowledged the God who had delivered His faithful servants and said,

"Praise be to the God of Shadrach, Meshach and Abednego, who has sent his angel and rescued his servants! They trusted in him and defied the king's command and were willing to give up their lives rather than serve or worship any god except their own God. Therefore I decree that the people of any nation or language who say anything against the God of Shadrach, Meshach and Abednego be cut into pieces and their houses be turned into piles of rubble, for no other god can save in this way."

Then the king promoted Shadrach, Meshach and Abednego in the province of Babylon (Daniel 3:28–30).

Later on, King Darius, after seeing the deliverance of Daniel from the lions' mouths, also offered up his acknowledgment to the God of Daniel, looking upon Him as superior to other gods (Daniel 6:26, 27). Both kings acknowledged that Yahweh is all-powerful and can protect His people from their enemies.

God's deliverance of His people in the past gives us confidence in His power, love, and faithfulness. We know that He will stand by and support us in our time of trial by either bringing us out of the fiery furnace or leading us through it. As Daniel and the three friends had confidence in God, they became fearless of the king's wrath, regardless of the risk to their lives. This is an inspiration for us to do the same.

The deliverance of the three friends continues to be a powerful testimony to me and many others in our time. Here we are thousands of years from when the story happened. We might be a few miles or thousands of miles from where it happened, yet the story still speaks to us to encourage us to be faithful to God.

The pastor said to me, "God is speaking to your heart in a powerful way. You need to take a stand and make a decision for Jesus right now. If you don't now, you might never."

I said to him, "I want to make a decision for Jesus."

He responded, "Pray after me, and give your heart to Him."

For the first time in my life, I prayed and gave Jesus my heart. We both cried with joy and peace.

Then he urged me, "It's time for you to get baptized."

I responded, "I want to," and he proposed we do it the next Sabbath.

He said to me, "I am going to get the whole church to pray that God will deliver you from the fire, but be prepared to go into the fire."

As I left his house, I claimed the promise that by doing the will of God, Jesus would become my family—my mother, my father, my brother, my sister, and my friend (Matthew 12:50). I determined in my heart I would follow Him all the way, even to the point of carrying my own cross. He was worth it.

I went to the Adventist pastor filled with fear about what might happen to me, but left filled with hope and courage. As the psalmist said, I started the night with terror but ended with encouragement that God would be with me in my time of trouble. He would deliver me and honor me (see Psalm 91).

Competing voices

The following Sabbath was one of the hardest days of my life. My exams would start at 9:00 A.M., and the baptism was scheduled for 11:30 A.M. I woke up at 5:00 A.M., and I was paralyzed. I could not move. I reflected on my life. If I took the exams, I would not be faithful to God. If I skipped the exams and got baptized, I would lose the whole year. It was a tremendous struggle.

I heard a voice saying to me, "You have broken thousands of Sabbaths before, one more is not going to make much difference." Then I heard the voice of God saying, "It is not about the Sabbath. It is about Me. How much you love Me, how much you trust Me." Then I heard the first voice saying to me, "You do not want to lose a whole year because of missing a few hours." Then I heard the voice of God saying to me, "It is not about a few hours or a day, it's about eternity. What you are struggling with has eternal value and consequences." Then the first voice said, "Just go do it. God will understand. Just one more Sabbath, and you will have the whole year under your belt. The Lord will understand. After all, what difference does it make to break another Sabbath?" But then I heard the voice of God saying, "Just trust in Me. I will carry you through. Follow Me. Trust in Me. I will take care of you."

This struggle lasted for six and a half hours. At 11:30 A.M., the Lord won out and gave me the victory. So I got out of bed, put on some clothes, and took a bus to the church. I arrived at about 12:30 P.M. The worship service was over, but most of the people were still out in the foyer. When I arrived, they invited everyone back into the sanctuary, and I was baptized in the name of Jesus and started to keep my first Sabbath that same day. I did not go and take the exams, and I lost a year of schooling; but praise the Lord, I had gained Jesus, and that is the most important thing of all.

Consequently, for the same reason, I lost my second year at the university. I pleaded with my professors to allow me to take the exams on a different day rather than the Sabbath, but they wouldn't. Failing the two years meant the loss of the scholarship I had earned that would cover my four years of college education. I was kicked out of the university because they decided I was not worth spending any more money on.

Left for Dead

God's Rescue of My Life

And we know that in all things
God works for the good of those who love him,
who have been called according to his purpose.
—Romans 8:28

When my father saw what was happening to me, he thought I was crazy or under some kind of hypnotic spell. He became very angry and called all of our relatives to come to our house. The house was completely full. At least one hundred people were crammed into our living room. It was impossible to get all those people together for a family reunion, but when they heard I had decided to take Jesus seriously and start keeping His Sabbath the way He commanded, they all came to discourage me and talk me out of it.

Everybody talked to me at the same time.

"How can you do this?" my father shouted at me.

"Yes, you're crazy!" one of my uncles yelled.

"You're bringing shame to our family," my mother cried.

Voices shouted at me from all directions as my parents and relatives tried to talk me out of my new faith.

"How can you want to be a Seventh-day Adventist? That religion is a cult."

"It's a Jewish religion!"

"Are you out of your mind?"

I just stood there, confused and under severe tension. Finally, when my dad thought he was not getting anywhere with me and that I was not going to change my mind, he took off his shoes, threw them at me, and spit on me (a sign of inflicting shame, representing the ultimate way of disgracing an individual in the Middle East). Seeing this, my cousin Basher—whom I was very close to—felt that it was his duty to straighten me out. So he and one of my brothers, Wadallah, grabbed me under the arms, lifted me up, and began to punch me. As I endured the blows, I was pushed in all directions, much like a piñata.

Soon all the boys and men in the room joined in, beating and spitting on me from all directions. They pulled my hair and ears and shouted hateful words about how I was stupid and a disgrace to them. I knew that in my culture, breaking away from the family religion is like denying the family and it is not tolerated. The concept of honor and shame is very important in the Middle East, and because I had diverted from family tradition, I became a source of shame and disgrace for them.

Almost dead

That day, my relatives beat me until I was almost dead. Then they threw me—bleeding and hurting—into the street as a final act of the cleansing ceremony. When I landed on the pavement, I heard my father shout, "I don't want to see you again! Don't come back until you change your mind and forget about this crazy religion!" Then everything went black in front of my swollen eyes, and I lost consciousness.

The Lord spared my life. A few hours later, I came back to consciousness. I was on the street. It was dark and cold. I looked up into the skies, and I said, "Lord, if I am doing all of the right things, why are all of the wrong things happening to me?" Everything I was afraid would happen, happened. I lost my schooling and my family. It was very difficult to feel the rejection of my family, but then I heard the voice of God saying to me, "Maybe you lost everything, but now you have Me, and if you have Me, that is all that you need."

Then I said, "Lord, I feel like the whole world is against me."

The Lord responded, "But I am for you."

If Jesus is for us, it doesn't matter who is against us.

God will work it out

At that time, the Adventist church in Baghdad had approximately two hundred members. The Lord impressed upon me to go to the home of my friends Muneer and Selma, who had taken an interest in me. Whenever I went to church, they would come and talk to me, pray with me, encourage me, and sometimes study the Bible with me. Occasionally they invited me to their home to eat lunch with them. They were wonderful. This family took me in and took care of my needs. They provided for my physical needs and encouraged me emotionally and spiritually. They prayed with me, read the Bible, and shared the promises of God.

One of the promises that we read many times is the one found in Romans 8:28: "And we know that in all things God works for the good of those who love him, who have been called according to his purpose."

Muneer and Selma pointed out to me that in the Greek, the text does not say, "We know," but says something stronger and more emphatic. It says, "We are convinced beyond any shadow of a doubt that God works out all things together for good to those who love Him." These promises flooded my heart with peace and assured me that, though abandoned by my family, Jesus was still there, very close to me.

Romans 8:28 is one of the most familiar verses in the Bible. The English Standard Version translates it, "And we know that for those who love God all things work together for good, for those who are called according to his purpose." All things don't just happen to work out for good on their own. Rather, God providentially works all things together for good for His people according to His purpose.

What Romans 8:28 says is that every one of God's providences eventually works "to the spiritual good of those who love God—in breaking them off from sin, bringing them nearer to God, weaning them from the world, and fitting them for heaven."[1]

In Romans 8:18, Paul reminds his readers "that the suffering of this present time are not worthy to be compared with the glory which shall be revealed in us" (NKJV). Skipping down to verses 26 and 27, we read:

"In the same way, the Spirit helps us in our weakness. We do not know what we ought to pray for, but the Spirit himself intercedes for us through wordless groans. And he who searches our hearts knows the mind of the Spirit, because the Spirit intercedes for God's people in accordance with the will of God."

I wanted to hear these encouraging words repeatedly, "If God is for us, who can be against us? He who did not spare his own Son, but gave him up for us all—how will he not also, along with him, graciously give us all things?" (verses 31, 32). And I love the way the apostle Paul ended this section about the love of God:

> Who shall separate us from the love of Christ? Shall trouble or hard-ship or persecution or famine or nakedness or danger or sword? As it is written: "For your sake we face death all day long; we are consid-ered as sheep to be slaughtered." No, in all these things we are more than conquerors through him who loved us. For I am convinced that neither death nor life, neither angels nor demons, neither the present nor the future, nor any powers, neither height nor depth, nor any-thing else in all creation, will be able to separate us from the love of God that is in Christ Jesus our Lord (verses 35–39).

Here, "Paul is showing that no matter how difficult the trial, even to the point of martyrdom, God's love for us is a rock-solid foundation. Whatever the trial, by faith, not by feelings, we must come back to God's love for us in Christ Jesus our Lord."[2]

Thus, "God's great love for us is not diminished or terminated by our failures, shortcomings, or sins, since it is rooted in God's choosing us before the foundation of the world. His love is not threatened or undermined by the worst adversities or trials imaginable. The greatest proof of His love was at the cross."[3] He died for us while we were still sinners. This is the ultimate demonstration of love (Romans 5:8).

These promises are not meant to assure us of success as we chase our secu-lar dreams. Instead, Paul is writing encouragement to believers who under-stood the cost of following Jesus. In Christ, we are more than conquerors.

Paul's words reflected his own experience with Christ. While our trials will be different from Paul's (see 2 Corinthians 11:23–28), challenges will arise throughout our lives. Knowing this, Paul encourages his readers to claim the promise of God's love and ever-present help in our lives.

When I went through those difficult times of persecution and trials, I felt like a mountain climber tied to my guide, Jesus Christ. Though the route was treacherous and I often slipped, I did not fall to my death because of the rope. Christ is our Guide who never slips, and the rope that ties us securely to Him is His great love for us, as seen on the cross.

1. Matthew Henry, *Concise Commentary on the Whole Bible*, s.v. "Romans 8:28," Bible Hub, http://biblehub.com/commentary/mhc/romans/8.htm.

2. Steven J. Cole, "The Triumph of God's Love (Romans 8:35–39)," *Romans* (online lesson series), Bible.org, copyright 2011, https://bible.org/seriespage/lesson-56-triumph-god-s-love-romans-835-39.

3. Cole, "The Triumph of God's Love."

Coming Home

God's Presence Casts Out My Fears

Say to those with fearful hearts, "Be strong, do not fear;
your God will come, he will come with vengeance;
with divine retribution he will come to save you."

—Isaiah 35:4

When Muneer and Selma recognized that I had no future in my country, they suggested that I should go to study at Middle East College in Beirut, Lebanon. Any college I wanted to go to had to be recognized by Iraq in order for them to give me an exit visa and allow me to study outside of my country—and Middle East College was not recognized.

At that time, the war between the Arab countries and Israel started in 1973. Since Iraq was part of the Arab countries, they started to draft people and send them to fight against Israel without training or preparation. One day, I received a notice from the army that I had to go into the service in six weeks (since I was not in school, I had to go serve in the army). *Now I'm going into the army to face endless problems*, I thought. *How will I keep the Sabbath? What if I refuse to bear arms and fight? What if I don't come back alive?* I was very fearful about the consequences I would face in the army, so I turned to the Bible.

Fear can lead us to panic if we allow it to control us. As Debbie McDaniel states, "Fear is one of the enemy's most popular weapons he uses against us. Worry, anxiety, and fear can overwhelm us with a thick shadow of darkness, controlling our every move and decision. Fear can lead us to panic if we allow it to control us. There is so much crazy going on around us today—wars, conflicts, persecution, violence, crime, natural disasters, terrorism, economic uncertainty, unemployment, divisions, disease, and death. We fear for our children's future, our families, our financial future, and our safety."[1]

To combat the fear for my life and my future, I read texts about fear in the Bible. The more I studied and claimed these texts, the easier it was to escape the feelings of fear and panic.

There are more than forty verses in the Bible to remind us that God is in control and that He is the One who casts out our fears and anxiety. God says, "Fear not. I will walk with you. I will stay with you. I will defeat your enemy. I will deliver you."

Most of these verses refer to God's presence. The Bible tells us repeatedly that His presence give us confidence and assurance that He is in control and that nothing is beyond His power and grace. He can take care of us. He can deliver us and save us. He gives us stability, hope, and joy. Acts 2:25–28 says,

> David said about him: "I saw the Lord always before me. Because he is at my right hand, I will not be shaken. Therefore my heart is glad and my tongue rejoices; my body also will rest in hope, because you will not abandon me to the realm of the dead, you will not let your holy one see decay. You have made known to me the paths of life; you will fill me with joy in your presence."

Here are some other Bible texts that I cherished:

- "Peace I leave with you; my peace I give you. I do not give to you as the world gives. Do not let your hearts be troubled and do not be afraid" (John 14:27).
- "I sought the Lord, and he answered me; he delivered me from all my fears" (Psalm 34:4).
- "The Lord is with me; I will not be afraid. What can mere mortals do to me?" (Psalm 118:6).

These Bible promises encouraged me to trust God with my life, and I learned to lean on Him when confronted by fear. Focusing on God's promises instead of my fear reduced the negative influences in my life and enabled my faith to grow stronger. "So do not fear, for I am with you; do not be dismayed, for I am your God. I will strengthen you and help you; I will uphold you with my righteous right hand" (Isaiah 41:10).

An offer I could refuse

By that time, my father knew that I was alive and living with this Adventist family. He also found out I had received the notice to serve in the army, so he sent me a letter saying, "I will accept you back home if you renounce your faith. Just forget about the whole mess you got yourself in, and we will accept you back. We will even arrange for you to go outside the country to study and avoid going into the army."

I was tempted to take my dad up on his offer, but praise the Lord for the community of faith that prayed for me and encouraged me to stay faithful to God. Almost every member of that church came and prayed with me personally and reminded me of verses in the Bible about faithfulness. I would not have been able to stay faithful without their encouragement, prayers, and support. Later I learned that the apostle Paul encourages us fifty-nine times to pray for one another, encourage one another, forgive one another, and love one another.

A tale of two sons

After receiving my father's message and facing the real possibility of having to bear arms and fight in the army, I reflected on the past few months of my life. I had lost everything—family, friends, a scholarship, and an education. I could not legally leave the country and go somewhere else to study. Instead, I was going into the army to face more challenges. I was down and discouraged. But in the midst of all of this, the promise that sustained me was Isaiah 59:1: "Surely the arm of the LORD is not too short to save, nor his ear too dull to hear." God, who is faithful to His promises, heard my prayers and extended His arm to solve my difficulties.

My neighbor, who was my best friend, was drafted into the army in the first wave. I was going to go in the second wave. However, in less than one week, the news came back that he was killed. My mother went to his memorial service. The death of my neighbor affected my mother so deeply that she wanted to see me very badly. She went home and said to my father, "I do not care whatever my son is, whether he is an Adventist or not . . . at least he is alive. I want him to come back home." It took some convincing, but eventually, my father allowed me to return home.

About a week after the memorial service for my neighbor, I came back home. The reception I received from my mom was very warm. She cried when she saw me, and she hugged and kissed me. The reception I received from my dad was cold and reserved. My brothers just watched.

That evening, we had a family meeting. My dad insisted that I needed to give him a good reason for why I did what I did. He was a businessman and acted in a professional manner most of the time. He said to me, "What drove you to lose two years of schooling and a scholarship that covered four years? You had the potential of a wonderful education and future. Why did you do what you did?"

I answered, "I did it out of love for Jesus. Jesus says if we love Him, we will keep His commandments [John 14:15]."

Those who love Jesus, who are born again, who have their spiritual sight fixed on Him and see His glory, will do everything to obey and honor Him. Those who are filled and anointed by the Holy Spirit, who have God's love in their hearts, having enjoyed communion with Him, will love Him above everything else and sacrifice everything for Him. All the followers of Jesus did that, from Abraham to Daniel, to the disciples, and all the way to our time. That is what God wants from us.

Christ is our Lord and Savior, Creator and Redeemer, and the Head of the church. As such, He has the right to issue out His commands, "If you love me, keep my commands" (John 14:15).

The meeting lasted more than an hour, but I was not sure anything productive came out of it. I did not think they really understood why I did what I did.

Midnight walk

It was about ten thirty on the first night I came home. I was already in bed asleep when the cousin and brother who had started the beating a few months earlier woke me up and said, "We need to go for a walk." I was scared. I thought they had found a way to kill me and get away with it, so I refused, but they forced me.

I was filled with fear, not knowing what would happen to me. I thought, *This is going to be the end. They are going to take me somewhere and kill me.*

---

1. Debbie McDaniel, "33 Verses About Fear and Anxiety to Remind Us: God Is in Control," *Family Features* (blog), 94.9 KLTY, accessed January 29, 2018, http://klty.com/content /family/33-verses-about-fear-and-anxiety-to-remind-us-god-is-in-control.

Midnight Walk

God's Revelation of Himself

The LORD said to Samuel, "Behold, I am about to do a thing in Israel at which both ears of everyone who hears it will tingle."
—1 Samuel 3:11, NASB

The New Testament is full of examples of God surprising His followers. One of the greatest New Testament surprises occurred when God took Saul, the persecutor, and turned him into Paul, the apostle of Jesus. As Melanie Newton declares, "Our God likes surprises. He does the unexpected as well as the expected in our lives."[1]

The book of Acts describes the spread of the gospel beyond the Jewish nation. Once again, God surprised His church by pouring out the Holy Spirit on a Roman centurion and his household. Through this surprise, God opened the way for Gentiles to be accepted as Christ-followers.

One day, I went on a midnight walk with one of my brothers and a cousin. I had no idea what was going to happen. It started one way and ended up completely different. "'For my thoughts are not your thoughts, neither are your ways my ways,' declares the LORD. 'As the heavens are higher than the earth, so are my ways higher than your ways and my thoughts than your thoughts'" (Isaiah 55:8, 9).

That night, I experienced the joy of waiting on God and watching what He does!

Bedroom intruders

Here I was, the first night after coming back home, and my brother and my cousin came into my bedroom and forced me to go on a walk with them. I protested, but they would not accept my refusal.

We walked about four miles to a park. By the time we got to the park, it was about midnight. I attempted to run away from them, but they ran after me, captured me, as one held on to my left arm and the other to my right arm. They forced me to the middle of the park and then stopped. I thought this was the end, so I started to pray and submit my life into the hands of God. I anticipated a knife stab or a shot. I closed my eyes and started to pray.

Three minutes went by, nothing happened. Six minutes, nothing happened. Ten minutes, nothing happened. Then my cousin broke the silence, saying, "Look, we saw what happened to you. We saw how everyone humiliated you, spit on you, and beat you. Why? You are either crazy to go through what you went through, or you have something we'd like to have too."

From darkness to light

Their request for an explanation gave me the opportunity to share with them what I had learned in my study of the Bible. I told them about the love of Jesus, the sacrifice He made on the cross, and His desire for us to accept His sacrifice. I talked to them about our condition as sinners and how desperately we are in need of a Savior. I told them that when I accepted Jesus into my heart, I felt peace, hope, and significance, and I felt like a new man in Christ. The gospel is the good news that God is restoring our broken lives through the death and resurrection of Jesus Christ.

I asked them the biggest question of all: "If you died today, do you have the assurance that your eternal life is secure with God?"

They said they had no idea, and I said something like this to them: "God loves you, even though He knows everything about you. He knows our secret sins, even when we think we're getting away with it. You've heard of the Ten Commandments, like 'Thou shalt not kill.' Have you ever murdered anyone? Jesus Christ says you have. Jesus said if you call someone a fool, or you're angry without cause, you've committed murder in your heart—in God's eyes.

Murderers will not inherit the kingdom of God. Do you ever get angry? We're all guilty."

I went on to say, "God did something to give us eternal life because He loves us. He must judge sin because He is just. Somebody is going to pay. Two thousand years ago, the Creator of the universe became a man—Jesus Christ. He lived a perfect life and urged us to repent, forsake our old lives and live a new life in Him. When He went to the cross, He was innocent. He shed His blood for your sins and mine. He suffered pain and ridicule on the cross. It was more than physical torture. It was the feeling of our guilt and shame on Himself. He took our place in death on that cross so you and I could go free. He died so we might live and have eternity. Three days later, He rose from the dead. Nobody else ever did that. Only Jesus Christ has the power to overcome death."

Continuing, I said, "You come before the judgment seat of God full of rebellion and mistakes. Because of His justice, He cannot dismiss your sin, but because of His love, He cannot dismiss you. So in an act that stunned the universe, He punished His Son on the cross for your sins. God's justice and love are equally honored. And you, God's creation, are forgiven. As the Bible says, 'God has a way to make people right with him without the law, and He has now shown us that way which the law and the prophets told us about. God makes people right with Himself through their faith in Jesus Christ' [Romans 3:21, 22]."

I appealed to them at the end. "Here is salvation: Admit to God that you've sinned against Him and deserve to die. Humble yourself. Agree with God that you are a sinner. Turn from your sins and your selfishness to God—that's repentance—and trust Jesus Christ for salvation. Jesus wants to save you for eternity, and that includes changing the rest of your life—to live righteously. Eternal life isn't just for the future. It's for right now—today! Surrender your life to Him, and He will give you a better life. God will make you a new person and give you the gift of everlasting life. He loves you."

Enriching our lives

One of the questions they asked me was if the Sabbath was for the Jews. I explained that God gave us the Sabbath at Creation. Genesis 2:2, 3 shows that people kept the Sabbath long before there were any Jews. It was given to the Israelites before Sinai when God commanded His people not to gather manna on the seventh day (see Exodus 16:22–26). Then it was commanded again at Sinai. "For in six days the LORD made the heavens and the earth, the sea, and all that is in them, but he rested on the seventh day. Therefore the LORD blessed the Sabbath day and made it holy" (Exodus 20:11). According to Isaiah, the Sabbath will continue in the world to come: " 'As the new heavens and the new earth that I make will endure before me,' declares the LORD, 'so will your name and descendants endure. From one New Moon to another and from one Sabbath to another, all mankind will come and bow down before me,' says the LORD" (Isaiah 66:22, 23). The Sabbath is part of the eternal Ten Commandments. It was sanctified at Creation, and according to Scripture, it will be part of our worship today and in heaven.

In the New Testament, there is no commandment to nullify the keeping of the Sabbath. Jesus kept it. "He went to Nazareth, where he had been brought up, and on the Sabbath day he went into the synagogue, as was his custom. He stood up to read" (Luke 4:16). The disciples kept it. "As Paul and Barnabas were leaving the synagogue, the people invited them to speak further about these things on the next Sabbath" (Acts 13:42). Jesus even urged His disciples to pray that their escape from Jerusalem would not be on the Sabbath. "Pray that your flight will not take place in winter or on the Sabbath." (Matthew 24:20).

I explained to them that God gave us the Ten Commandments to enrich our lives. They help us to relate to one another and God in a healthy way. God gave us the Sabbath as a day of rest, to focus on Him and be with our families. Obedience to God in regard to the Sabbath is not so much about keeping a day, but about being fully committed to His will for our lives.

I also mentioned to them that there are about 1,100 references to the Sabbath in the Bible, and not one of them says to break it. They are all very positive about how the Sabbath was given to us to build a relationship with God and to worship Him. Therefore, the Sabbath was never meant to be done away with. I also explained that obedience to God is for our own good. God created us to be faithful to Him, and when we do that, we will receive rich and lasting blessings.

Revelation of my humiliation

We were there until sunrise. At six o'clock in the morning, my brother Wadallah gave his heart to Jesus Christ. Prior to that, he was a secular man who worshiped money, but since that day, he has been a worshiper of Jesus. My cousin Basher, who started the beating, later became the pastor of the Seventh-day Adventist church in Bagdad, Iraq. Before Basher became a pastor, he was working in a factory that took blood from slaughtered animals and converted it into fertilizers.

As a result of Wadallah and Basher sharing their faith and excitement about the Lord, many more members of my family have joined the church, including my other brother, Janan, his family, and several other cousins and their families.

While I was out on the street, after all of these bad things had happened to me, I asked myself, *Am I doing the right thing?* When I came back home, God revealed to me that He had used this experience for His purpose and His glory. It was through this experience from darkness into light that my brother and my cousin came to know Him.

When I went through the persecution and humiliation and losing two years of schooling, I did not grow bitter. I did not hate my family or the professors of the university. I knew they did all of this because of their culture, tradition, and concern for me. I was at times tempted to hate them, but I decided to pray for them instead. God answered my prayer, and several members of my family came to know the Lord.

God always awakens in the hearts of people an interest in Him as they see others go through difficult times and yet stand firm for the Lord. Paul was surprised by the unwavering commitment of Stephen, who was willing to die for the cause of Jesus. That was one of the factors that eventually turned him around. My brother and cousin were surprised by my enduring faithfulness, and that brought them to inquire of the Lord and eventually become fully committed followers of Jesus Christ.

Fake news

It was the news about the death of my neighbor that allowed me to come back home. Later, my neighbor was found—alive! It was a case of mistaken identity. But the Lord used the bad news of his so-called death to bring the good news of salvation to my family, beginning with a late-night walk with my brother and cousin.

---

1. Melanie Newton, "6. The God of the Unexpected," *Radical Acts: The Fire of the Spirit Erupting Though Believers* (study series), Bible.org, January 6, 2012, https://bible.org /seriespage/6-god-unexpected.

Stepping Out in Faith

God's Sovereignty Over Everything

Immediately the boy's father exclaimed,
"I do believe; help me overcome my unbelief!"

—Mark 9:24

When my cousin Basher became an Adventist, he was working in a factory that took blood from slaughtered animals and converted it into fertilizer. As he was growing in his relationship with the Lord, he also became convinced about keeping the Sabbath. Iraq operated on a system of six days of work and one day off on Friday.

Walking on the water

One day, as he was reading the Bible, he came across the story of Peter walking on water. The story begins with Jesus making His disciples get into the boat and go to the other side of the Sea of Galilee. He then goes up to the side of the mountain and starts praying. However, at about three o'clock in the morning, the boat, a considerable distance from shore, encountered stormy waves on the sea. It was at that time that Jesus came walking on the water to meet them:

> When the disciples saw him walking on the lake, they were terrified. "It's a ghost," they said, and cried out in fear.

But Jesus immediately said to them: "Take courage! It is I. Don't be afraid."

"Lord, if it's you," Peter replied, "tell me to come to you on the water."

"Come," he said.

Then Peter got down out of the boat, walked on the water and came toward Jesus. But when he saw the wind, he was afraid and, beginning to sink, cried out, "Lord, save me!"

Immediately Jesus reached out his hand and caught him. "You of little faith," he said, "why did you doubt?"

And when they climbed into the boat, the wind died down. Then those who were in the boat worshiped him, saying, "Truly you are the Son of God" (Matthew 14:26–33).

Basher specifically noticed that Peter stepped out of the boat in faith and walked on the water.

We all know that God wants us to walk in faith. We all know that it is easy to walk in faith when there are no trials, pain, loss, or conflict—but that is not good enough. God needs to develop faith in us that will endure. He wants us to grow strong in faith. The only possible way that He can do that is to teach us to weather the storms that appear from nowhere in our lives.

Faith is a verb. It requires acting on what we know to be true based on Scripture. As we act, our faith will strengthen and grow in proportion to our step of obedience. When we act in faith, we will encounter trials, but through this experience we learn that God will never forsake us.

Going through a personal storm

Trials are a natural part of following Christ. Second Timothy 3:12 says, "In fact, everyone who wants to live a godly life in Christ Jesus will be persecuted." These trials come in a variety of shapes and sizes, and involve different aspects of our lives. Jesus never promised His followers an easy life. Instead, He promised to walk through life with them.

Even when trials appear to hide God's presence, if you're looking for Him and acknowledge that He can be there in the storm, you will walk on the stormy waters of life and defeat them by His presence. "Be strong and courageous. Do not be afraid or terrified because of them, for the LORD your

God goes with you; he will never leave you nor forsake you" (Deuteronomy 31:6; see Hebrews 13:5).

Basher felt that he needed to step out in faith, go to his boss, and ask him to give him the Sabbath off. He knelt down and prayed that God would give him the courage and the words he needed to say.

Double duty production

The Lord gave him a very specific thing to say, and the following day, Basher went to his boss and said to him, "I'm a follower of Jesus, and He commanded us to keep the Sabbath day holy. I want to be faithful to Him and honor Him and keep the Sabbath, so I am respectfully requesting you give me the Sabbath day off."

His boss replied, "That's impossible. There is no way I can do that. Everyone will come to me and ask me the same thing. There are fifty other workers working a machine like you, and I cannot accommodate."

My cousin said to him (this is what the Lord told him to say), "Give me a chance of four weeks, and at the end of every week, if my machine does not produce more fertilizer in five days than it will produce in six days, fire me. But if the machine does produce more, keep me on."

His boss said, "How is this going to happen?"

Basher told him, "I really don't know, but I am going to pray about it and let God take care of the rest."

At the end of the first week, Basher's machine produced in five days double of what the machine was supposed to produce in six days. The same thing happened in the second week, the third week, and the fourth week. The boss came to him and said, "I am more than willing to give you the Sabbath day off as long as you keep up the same level of production." The other workers, seeing that Basher was taking two days off, went to the boss and asked for the same thing. He said to them, "Basher's machine produces double in five days what the others do in six days. If your machines can do the same as Basher's, I will give you two days off also."

Most of Basher's fifty coworkers were Muslim. They went to him and asked, "How did you do this? What kind of modifications did you employ to make the machine do double?"

He said, "I didn't make any modifications. I prayed about it, and God did the rest."

They said, "Tell us more about it. Why did you do that?"

He said, "God, out of love for us, gave us a day to rest, called the Sabbath, to worship and enjoy Him. After reading the Bible, I became convicted that I need to have that day to worship God. So I prayed to God, asking that He would help me to produce more in five days than what the machine could normally produce in six days. Because God is faithful and loves His children very much, He answered my prayers. He made my machine produce in five days double what it would normally do in six days."

Many coworkers wanted to know more about Basher's faith, his conviction about the Sabbath, and the power of God, which led him to give Bible studies, resulting in several conversions. Many people came to worship the Lord because of the faithfulness of one individual who stepped out of the boat and decided to be fully committed to Jesus Christ. When we step out of the boat, people will take notice, and some will come to declare Jesus to be the Son of God and worship Him.

Career change

About a year and a half after this incident, Basher felt a very strong call to the ministry. He went to Middle East College and studied theology. Then he returned to Baghdad to pastor the Adventist church, but during the United States' invasion of Iraq in 2003 (dubbed by the United States as Operation Iraqi Freedom), Basher went to Lebanon and pastored one of the churches there. As Basher was having his devotion one day in Lebanon, he asked himself, *Who is going to minister to the people of Iraq?* He decided to go back to Iraq to minister. He and his family started a small church in Duhok, Iraq (which is on the border between Kurdistan and the state of Nineveh, close to the border of Turkey).

So many times, we look at the course of our lives and feel discouraged because our plans are failing, because we have problem after problem. We are upset because, for some reason or another, we do not understand God's plans. At these times, we must look to Jesus, the Author and Perfecter of our faith (Hebrews 12:2). The Lord used all of my problems for His glory, for my own good, and for the good of my family.

The God of Miracles

God's Answer to My Prayers

"Because he loves me," says the LORD, *"I will rescue him;*
I will protect him, for he acknowledges my name.
He will call on me, and I will answer him."
—Psalm 91:14, 15

The friends I had stayed with, Muneer and Selma, said to me, "You still have to go to college to postpone the problem of being drafted into the army." Then they continued, "For forty years, the church in Iraq has been trying to get Middle East College to be recognized by the state, and they have failed. They have tried everything: connection, influence, and even bribery, but nothing has worked." Finally Muneer and Selma said, "Let's try prayer." Not that the church had not prayed before, but they had not prayed with intensity, passion, and earnestness. That is what Muneer and Selma wanted to do this time.

Fervent prayer
The following Sabbath, they had a meeting during Sabbath School. Muneer and Selma said to the church, "We need to do something to get Middle East College recognized. We suggest trying prayer."

Someone spoke up, "We tried that before."

They responded, "We did, but this time, we are going to pray with intensity and with all of our hearts. Remember, 'Therefore confess your sins to each other and pray for each other so that you may be healed. The prayer of a righteous person is powerful and effective' [James 5:16]."

The King James Versions reads, "Confess your faults one to another, and pray one for another, that ye may be healed. The effectual fervent prayer of a righteous man availeth much." The Greek word for "availeth much," or as other translations say, "accomplishes" or "empowers," means strengthening someone in terms of health and personal strength. Also, the word means to give power, or to give extraordinary power, to get things accomplished.[1] Prayer has a strengthening influence, giving us health and empowering us to do supernatural things. "And I will do whatever you ask in my name, so that the Father may be glorified in the Son. You may ask me for anything in my name, and I will do it" (John 14:13, 14).

Then they quoted Ellen White:

Our Heavenly Father waits to bestow upon us the fullness of His blessing. It is our privilege to drink largely at the fountain of boundless love. What a wonder it is that we pray so little! God is ready and willing to hear the sincere prayer of the humblest of His children. . . .

. . . Why should the sons and daughters of God be reluctant to pray, when prayer is the key in the hand of faith to unlock heaven's storehouse, where are treasured the boundless resources of Omnipotence?[2]

During the church service, an announcement was made that they had decided to devote all the following weekend, starting on Friday evening, to prayer and fasting.

On the following Friday night, about fifty members went into the basement of the Adventist church to pray, worship, and fast until Sunday afternoon (influenced in that area by Jonah's three-day fast). On Sabbath, the rest of the church joined them.

The structure of the meeting was to read Scripture and pray over it. Here are some of the scriptures they used:

• "Look to the Lord and his strength; seek his face always" (1 Chronicles 16:11).

- "Then you will call on me and come and pray to me, and I will listen to you" (Jeremiah 29:12).

- "Truly I tell you, if you have faith as small as a mustard seed, you can say to this mountain, 'Move from here to there,' and it will move. Nothing will be impossible for you" (Matthew 17:20).

- "Therefore I tell you, whatever you ask for in prayer, believe that you have received it, and it will be yours" (Mark 11:24).

- "So I say to you: Ask and it will be given to you; seek and you will find; knock and the door will be opened to you. For everyone who asks receives; the one who seeks finds; and to the one who knocks, the door will be opened. Which of you fathers, if your son asks for a fish, will give him a snake instead? Or if he asks for an egg, will give him a scorpion? If you then, though you are evil, know how to give good gifts to your children, how much more will your Father in heaven give the Holy Spirit to those who ask Him!" (Luke 11:9–13).

- "And I will do whatever you ask in my name, so that the Father may be glorified in the Son. You may ask me for anything in my name, and I will do it" (John 14:13, 14).

- "And my God will meet all your needs according to the riches of his glory in Christ Jesus" (Philippians 4:19).

- "This is the confidence we have in approaching God: that if we ask anything according to his will, he hears us. And if we know that he hears us—whatever we ask—we know that we have what we asked of him" (1 John 5:14, 15).

In addition to praying over Scripture, they often gave quotations from Ellen G. White or their own personal testimonies of how God answered prayers in their own lives. Some of the Ellen G. White quotes included these:

- "The greatest blessing that God can give to man is the spirit of earnest prayer. All heaven is open before the man of prayer. . . . The ambassadors of Christ will have power with the people after they have, with earnest supplication, come before God."[3]

- "Jacob prevailed because he was persevering and determined. His experience testifies to the power of importunate prayer. It is now that we are to learn this lesson of prevailing prayer, of unyielding faith. The greatest victories to the church of Christ or to the individual Christian are not those that are gained by talent or education, by wealth or the favor of men. They are those victories that are gained in the audience chamber with God, when earnest, agonizing faith lays hold upon the mighty arm of power."[4]

- "Keep your wants, your joys, your sorrows, your cares, and your fears before God. You cannot burden Him; you cannot weary Him. He who numbers the hairs of your head is not indifferent to the wants of His children. 'The Lord is very pitiful, and of tender mercy.' James 5:11. His heart of love is touched by our sorrows and even by our utterances of them. Take to Him everything that perplexes the mind. Nothing is too great for Him to bear, for He holds up worlds, He rules over all the affairs of the universe. Nothing that in any way concerns our peace is too small for Him to notice. There is no chapter in our experience too dark for Him to read; there is no perplexity too difficult for Him to unravel. No calamity can befall the least of His children, no anxiety harass the soul, no joy cheer, no sincere prayer escape the lips, of which our heavenly Father is unobservant, or in which He takes no immediate interest. 'He healeth the broken in heart, and bindeth up their wounds.' Psalm 147:3. The relations between God and each soul are as distinct and full as though there were not another soul upon the earth to share His watchcare, not another soul for whom He gave His beloved Son."[5]

God is a competent Father. He can handle any problem you give Him. Nothing is beyond His ability or His resources. No request is too big or too small.

When my kids were little, it amazed me at everything they assumed I could do, such as fixing bicycles and toys. My kids expected me to know everything, to fix anything, and to be able to afford trips, summerhouses, and boats. As they grew up, they learned that their father had limited knowledge, limited energy, limited resources, limited skills—limited everything. However, our heavenly Father really can do anything. Ephesians 3:20 says, "Now all glory to God, who is able, through his mighty power at work within us, to accomplish infinitely more than we might ask or think" (NLT).

Yesterday's impossibilities are today's miracles. God specializes in doing the impossible! He is a competent Father.

A time to celebrate

On Tuesday of that week, the news came from the government that Middle East College was now recognized by the Department of Education in Iraq. Forty years of human effort failed miserably, but God answered their prayer almost immediately. It would be good for us to learn to present our needs to the Lord right away.

The following Sabbath, the church held a celebration. They cited Psalm 118:1–9:

> Give thanks to the LORD, for he is good;
>   his love endures forever.
> Let Israel say:
>   "His love endures forever."
> Let the house of Aaron say:
>   "His love endures forever."
> Let those who fear the LORD say:
>   "His love endures forever."
>
> When hard pressed, I cried to the LORD;
>   he brought me into a spacious place.
> The LORD is with me; I will not be afraid.
>   What can mere mortals do to me?
> The LORD is with me; He is my helper.
>   I look in triumph on my enemies.
>
> It is better to take refuge in the LORD
>   than to trust in humans.

> It is better to take refuge in the LORD
> than to trust in princes.

As David's heart was full of the goodness of God, our hearts were filled with joy caused by the miraculous answer to our prayers. Just as David loved to think, speak, and sing of the goodness of God, we also broke into praise of what God had done. The more our hearts are impressed with a sense of God's goodness, the more they will expand in all manner of praise, worship, and obedience.

The recognition of Middle East College gave me the opportunity to go and study there and avoid joining the Iraqi army. At that time, I still wanted to be an engineer, but Middle East College did not have that major. I planned on taking some general education classes there, then transferring to another university in Beirut to take engineering.

Later on, I came to the realization that the two years I had lost at the previous university proved to be a blessing for me. If I had taken the exams on Sabbath and passed, due to the amount of money the government would have spent on me, I would have been obligated to work Sabbaths for four years for them. Since they were no longer sponsoring me, I was able to study outside of the country.

---

1. "Ischyō," Blue Letter Bible, last modified January 1, 2018, https://www.blueletterbible.org/lang/lexicon/lexicon.cfm?Strongs=G2480&t=KJV.

2. Ellen G. White, *Steps to Christ* (Nampa, ID: Pacific Press®, 2000), 94, 95.

3. Ellen G. White, "Laboring in the Spirit of Christ," *The Advent Review and Sabbath Herald*, October 20, 1896.

4. Ellen G. White, *Patriarchs and Prophets* (Nampa, ID: Pacific Press®, 2002), 203.

5. White, *Steps to Christ*, 100.

The Lord Is My Refuge

God's Protection Over My Life

*But the Lord is faithful, and he will strengthen you
and protect you from the evil one.*
—2 Thessalonians 3:3

After I received the acceptance letter from Middle East College, I took a bus from Baghdad to Damascus, then on to Beirut, Lebanon, to begin the 1974–1975 school year. When I arrived in Lebanon, I was impressed by how beautiful the country was. Middle East College is on the eastern side of Beirut, halfway up the mountain in a very beautiful place that overlooks the city and the Mediterranean Sea.

Between a rock and a hard place

On the top of the mountain were the Christian Maronites—a branch of Christianity that reestablished full communion with the Catholic Church in the year 1182, after hundreds of years of isolation in the mountains of Lebanon. At the bottom of the mountain were the Muslim Shiites—a branch of Islam that holds the belief that the Islamic prophet Muhammad designated Ali ibn Abi Talib, Muhammad's son-in-law, as his successor.

The two camps did not get along well at all. From time to time, they shot rockets at each other. Some of these rockets fell on Middle East College's campus. This happened infrequently until the Lebanese civil war started in April of 1975. This war, between the Christians and Muslims, lasted for fifteen years from 1975 to 1990.

The first six months of my stay at Middle East College were very pleasant. It was a beautiful area, and the campus was multicultural. Students and professors came from all over the world. I worked in the bakery and delivered bread throughout the city. I was able to enjoy the view of the Mediterranean Sea as we made our deliveries.

Once the Lebanese civil war started, however, life was tense and fear was again a threat in my life for about a year and a half. During that time, I felt very strongly the protection of the Lord and His grace upon me.

He is my refuge

About that time, my mom started to read the Bible. Knowing the civil war was going on in Lebanon and that I was in a dangerous place, the Lord directed her to Psalm 91. Daily, she started to claim its promises on my behalf:

> Whoever dwells in the shelter of the Most High
>> will rest in the shadow of the Almighty.
> I will say of the LORD, "He is my refuge and my fortress,
>> my God, in whom I trust."
>
> Surely he will save you
>> from the fowler's snare
>> and from the deadly pestilence.
> He will cover you with his feathers,
>> and under his wings you will find refuge;
>> his faithfulness will be your shield and rampart (Psalm 91:1–4).

These are wonderful words of hope, comfort, and affirmation. They certainly provide encouragement for those who confess Jehovah as their God. They speak of God as the Protector of those who trust in Him. They promise that while many will suffer destruction, the one who has trusted in God, who has fled to Him for safety, will be delivered. Charles Spurgeon expands on this passage of Scripture.

The Omnipotent Lord will shield all those who dwell with him, they shall remain under his care as guests under the protection of their host. In the most holy place the wings of the cherubim were the most conspicuous objects, and they probably suggested to the psalmist the expression here employed. Those who commune with God are safe with him, no evil can reach them, for the outstretched wings of his power and love cover them from all harm. This protection is constant—they *abide* under it, and it is all-sufficient, for it is the shadow of *the Almighty*, whose omnipotence will surely screen them from all attack. No shelter can be imagined at all comparable to the protection of Jehovah's own shadow. The Almighty himself is where his shadow is, and hence those who dwell in his secret place are shielded by himself. What a shade in the day of noxious heat! What a refuge in the hour of deadly storm! Communion with God is safety. The more closely we cling to our Almighty Father, the more confident may we be.[1]

Sometimes God's protection appears to be absent, but He has promised, "Can a mother forget the baby at her breast and have no compassion on the child she has borne? Though she may forget, I will not forget you! See, I have engraved you on the palms of my hands; your walls are ever before me" (Isaiah 49:15, 16). The God who loves us with everlasting love will continually be a safe haven for His followers.

In Psalm 91:1, God invites His followers to make Him their permanent residence. Trials may disrupt our lives, but in Christ, our foundation will remain secure.

As we abide in Christ, we find rest in the "shadow of the Almighty" (Psalm 91:1). His shadow protects us from the worst heat of the trial.

Even when trials seem to surround us, God will not forsake His followers. True security is found in abiding in Jesus. There, in His "shadow," we find perfect peace.

Psalm 91 is full of God's promises to protect His people. " 'Because he loves me,' says the LORD, 'I will rescue him; I will protect him, for he acknowledges my name. He will call on me, and I will answer him; I will be with him in trouble, I will deliver him and honor him. With long life I will satisfy him and show him my salvation' " (verses 14–16).

This psalm gives us greater depth about what God will do for us. He will

- rescue,
- protect,
- respond,
- remain,
- deliver,
- honor,
- satisfy, and
- reveal.

God's promises will not fail. He will never forsake us.

My mom, from time to time, would write to me and tell me that she was claiming the promises of Psalm 91 on my behalf, so I started to read it too. The verses that really caught my attention were, "The LORD is my refuge," (verse 9) and, therefore, no harm will ever come upon me and no disaster will come near me (verse 10). "For he will command his angels concerning you to guard you in all your ways;" (verse 11).

Sniper bullets

I have experienced the fulfillment of these promises and the protection of God many times in Lebanon. One day, a friend and I took the time to study math together under some trees close to the dormitory. As we got stuck on a math problem, we drifted into talking about the civil war in Lebanon. We were fearful of this war and its close proximity. We decided to take the Bible and claim promises of protection, such as,

> But let all who take refuge in you be glad;
>> let them ever sing for joy.
> Spread your protection over them,
>> that those who love your name may rejoice in you" (Psalm 5:11).

Also,

> "My God is my rock, in whom I take refuge,
>> my shield and the horn of my salvation.
> He is my stronghold, my refuge and my savior—
>> from violent people you save me.

I called to the LORD, who is worthy of praise,
   and have been saved from my enemies" (2 Samuel 22:3, 4).

As we read these promises, we felt God's hands upon us, compelling us to move from where we were studying. Rather than sitting beneath the tree, we moved to stand behind the tree. The moment we moved, the bullets started coming in our direction from snipers. This lasted for two to three minutes, then stopped. When there was a cease-fire, we ran to the dorm. God was faithful to His promises and protected us.

A bomb in my bed

A few days later, I was sick with the flu and stayed in bed. I asked my room-mate to bring me breakfast. As I was eating my food, sitting on my bed, I felt a compelling urge to leave the room. It was like a voice speaking to me, "Get out!" Then I felt what I sensed was a hand holding my hand and taking me outside the room.

When I got to the common area inside the dormitory, I started to hear the sound of the artillery and the bombs going back and forth between the Muslims and the Christians. Then I heard a very loud explosion close to me, so I ducked, and then fell flat on my face.

A few minutes later, when everything calmed down, I wanted to know where that loud explosion came from. I went to my bedroom, and I saw that my bed was torn into millions of pieces. A bomb had come through the wall and exploded exactly where my bed had been. Again, God fulfilled the promises of Psalm 91 in my life and answered the prayers of my mom.

Later on when I arrived in Baghdad, my mother and I sat together and prayed this prayer:

"Dear God,
   Thank You for Your presence and protection. Thank You for hold-ing our lives in Your hands. Thank You for the comfort and hope we find in Your promises.
   Please open our eyes to the ways You lead and guide us each day.
   In Jesus' name, amen."

While I was living in Lebanon, we lived in fear most of the time—

hard-pressed between Christians and Muslims. It was dangerous to be in the dorm. It was dangerous to be on campus. It was dangerous to go into town. The only thing that kept us going was claiming the promises of God. The Word of God came to Joshua, "Yes, be bold and strong! Banish fear and doubt! For remember, the Lord your God is with you wherever you go" (Joshua 1:9, TLB). This text also came to us to give us comfort and peace.

Ellen White captured God's protection for His children in these inspiring words:

> The daily record of disasters shows that there is no safety anywhere. Even in our homes we are in danger; for storms, floods, and fire are sweeping off thousands, while earthquakes are destroying additional thousands. If there ever was a time when we should be sober and watch unto prayer, it is now. Our lives are safe only when hid with Christ in God. We need every day to purify ourselves even as He is pure. There is always hope for us in God. Faith is our defense, for it connects our human weakness with divine power.[2]

During difficult times, we must find our safety in God.

---

1. C. H. Spurgeon, *The Treasury of David*, vol. 4, *Psalms 79–103* (London, 1874), 231.

2. Ellen G. White, "Notes of Travel," *The Advent Review and Sabbath Herald*, January 29, 1884.

No Safe Places

God's Presence Is Everywhere

The LORD is my shepherd, I lack nothing.
He makes me lie down in green pastures.

—Psalm 23:1

Due to the civil war in Beirut, Lebanon, I was forced to seek an education elsewhere. One day, Mark, a classmate from the United States, asked me, "Do you still want to be an engineer?"

"Yes," I responded.

He said, "Go to Walla Walla College in the state of Washington in the United States."

My first reaction was to respond, "Who in his right mind would go to Walla Walla?" In Arabic, *Walla Walla* sounds like, "The Place of the Double Curse." The meaning of names is important in Arabic, so I thought this must be a bad place!

He explained to me that it had nothing to do with curses. Walla Walla was a Native American name for "The Place of Many Waters." This area is located near several bodies of water.

"How much does it cost to attend Walla Walla College?" I asked.

"About eight thousand dollars a year," Mark replied.

"That means I would need a minimum of thirty-two thousand dollars to attend Walla Walla College and graduate. I don't have any money. There is no way for me to go over there," I responded.

Mark said to me, "If God wants you to go to Walla Walla, He will provide a way for you to go there. Remember, 'And my God will meet all your needs according to the riches of his glory in Christ Jesus' [Philippians 4:19]. And, 'For every animal of the forest is mine, and the cattle on a thousand hills' [Psalm 50:10]."

Then he cited several more examples from the Bible about how God cares for our needs. God counts the hairs on our heads. He cares about the sparrows and the lilies of the field. Luke 12:24 says, "Consider the ravens: They do not sow or reap, they have no storeroom or barn; yet God feeds them. And how much more valuable you are than birds!"

Mark said, "It is easy for the Lord to supply thirty-two thousand. Let's pray about it."

So we prayed over this situation. After several days of prayer, he said, "I was impressed by God to contact my father in the US to work on finding a sponsor for you."

Emergency evacuation

About that same time, the administration at Middle East College felt that everyone should leave the country for their own safety because the civil war was nearing the campus. The Maronite Christian militia was using the campus as a stronghold. The frequency of the bombing increased as the Shiite Muslims fired shots at the Christian militia.

At the beginning of 1975, the administration at Middle East College decided to close the school. We were supposed to leave on a Tuesday at 5:00 P.M. We got to the bus stop at 4:00 P.M. and waited nervously. As we waited, we heard on the radio that the fighting had intensified in the city of Beirut. A few minutes before 5:00 P.M., we were told that the buses were running late and had rescheduled the departure for 9:00 P.M.

There were about eighty students and forty faculty and staff left from every corner of the world at Middle East College. About 5:00 P.M., the stranded group decided to go to the cafeteria on the opposite side of campus to eat. While we were eating, we started to hear the bombing. It felt very close to us. One of the bombs came through the front wall of the cafeteria and exploded inside. Fortunately, it exploded in a place where no one was sitting.

We immediately went into the bomb shelter connected to the cafeteria, split into several groups, and started to pray as we claimed promises of protection from the Bible. We stayed there until about 8:00 P.M., when the bombing stopped completely, and we felt safe enough to leave. We left the bomb shelter and went to the place where we were supposed to meet the buses. The place was completely destroyed, including the immediate area around the bus stop. In fact, we saw huge craters where the bombs had landed. Immediately we knew why the buses were delayed—God had allowed it. He had protected us. If we had been waiting in the location where the buses were to pick us up between 5:00 P.M. and 8:00 P.M., during the heaviest bombing time, we would all be dead.

God saved our lives. He is faithful to His promises of protecting His people. In the day that God delivered David, he sang this song found in Psalm 18:1–6:

I love you, Lord, my strength.

The Lord is my rock, my fortress and my deliverer;
    my God is my rock, in whom I take refuge,
    my shield and the horn of my salvation, my stronghold.

I called to the Lord, who is worthy of praise,
    and I have been saved from my enemies.
The cords of death entangled me;
    the torrents of destruction overwhelmed me.
The cords of the grave coiled around me;
    the snares of death confronted me.

In my distress I called to the Lord;
    I cried to my God for help.
From his temple he heard my voice;
    my cry came before him, into his ears. (See also 2 Samuel 22:2–7.)

Those who receive mercies and protection from God ought to give Him the glory also. God will preserve all of His people. "The Lord will rescue me from every evil attack and will bring me safely to his heavenly kingdom. To him be glory for ever and ever. Amen" (2 Timothy 4:18). Ellen G. White writes, "We may know that if our life is hid with Christ in God, when we are brought into trial because of our faith, Jesus will be with us."[1]

As we were standing in front of a large crater, one individual started reciting Psalm 23, and all of us joined in. "Even though I walk through the darkest valley, I will fear no evil, for you are with me; your rod and your staff, they comfort me" (Psalm 23:4). The president of the university offered a prayer of thanksgiving to God for protecting and saving our lives.

The great escape

Then we got on the bus to travel to the harbor to catch our ship. We saw more destruction on both sides of the highway—buildings and people. Even if we had escaped the destruction at the bus stop, we would have been destroyed on the way to the harbor if our buses had arrived on time.

All of us were put on a sheep cargo ship (not a Norwegian Cruise Line ship) and went all the way to Tartus, Syria. What normally would take half a day to travel from Beirut to Tartus by ship took us almost three days because we went far out to sea to avoid the bombs and the snipers closer to shore. We stood up the whole time, crammed among many people. We got sunburned, and there was not enough food to eat or water to drink.

In Tartus, the concerned immigration officers interrogated us individually because there were so many nationalities trying to enter Syria. At the end of the day, they decided not to allow us to stay in the country, so they put us on the same cargo ship and sent us to Cyprus. That took another three days—without food and water, cramped like sardines in the ship. When we arrived at Cyprus, we stayed in a building owned by the Adventist Church conference there for several days, trying to find flights to our separate destinations. Finally, after staying there for five days, I was able to get a flight from Cyprus to Baghdad.

I went back to Baghdad, Iraq, and I shared with Muneer and Selma my desire to go to Walla Walla College in the United States. I told them about my discouragement that since I did not have money, the United States would not give me an entry visa, and Iraq would not give me permission to leave—and I might have to serve in the army.

How would God solve all of these problems? What was He going to do?

---

1. Ellen G. White, *Our High Calling*, (Hagerstown, MD: Review and Herald®, 2000), 357.

Prayer Over the Impossible

God's Power to Perform Miracles

*"Truly I tell you, if you have faith as small as a mustard seed,
you can say to this mountain, 'Move from here to there,'
and it will move. Nothing will be impossible for you."*
—Matthew 17:20

After I left Lebanon and went back to Iraq in 1976, I had a major crisis in my life. During that time, I had already lost two years of education because of the Sabbath and my schooling situation in Iraq, which caused me to leave the country and attend Middle East College. Because of the civil war, I was forced to go back home to Iraq. What I really wanted was to go to Walla Walla College to study engineering.

Unfortunately, I was faced with four major problems. First off, I had no money. At that time, the cost of Walla Walla was seven to eight thousand dollars a year, and I had a total of about five dollars saved up. I was told that I was totally out of my mind to even think of going to Walla Walla College. There would be no way for me to afford it. It was impossible.

The second major problem was the strained relationship between Iraq and the US. The Iraqi government had strictly forbidden people from going to the US for any reason, and the US was not giving visas to Iraqi citizens. For many years, there has been a mutual distrust between the two governments.

The third issue was also related to the Iraqi government—mandatory army service. Since I was not in school, the Iraqi army had sent a notice that I was required to enlist in the army.

The fourth problem that seemed to have no solution was that I needed to find someone to guarantee that I would come back to Iraq if I went to Walla Walla. If I didn't come back, this person would have to pay $10,000. I didn't know of anyone who would be willing and able to take on this responsibility.

As I reflected on these problems, they seemed impossible to resolve. My heart sank. What could I do about it?

Stopping short

Muneer and Selma said that the only solution for those problems was to pray—a lot! We have a God that can do the impossible. He demonstrated that in the Bible, in history, and in our lives.

If we know that God can do the impossible, why don't we pray more? Too often, we start praying then gradually lose our momentum. We find that we're repeating requests and losing our focus. We get tired of waiting and asking for the same thing repeatedly. Eventually, we say, "Why bother?" and quit praying.

On the one hand we know that God loves us and responds to our prayers. But on the other hand we struggle to realize this truth in our individual walk with God. When our hearts doubt God's love and care, we don't pray and ask Him to fulfill our pressing needs. We must answer the question: Is God able to care for my needs? Because if He *isn't*, all the good will in heaven and earth makes no difference.

The Bible clearly describes God's willingness to care for His children. But He waits for us to recognize His power and ask for His help.

Many times, I told myself, "I don't have any good models of persevering prayer, and I don't have the time to pray properly." In response, God showed me the truth behind these excuses—I was doubting His goodness and care. Repentance and confession brought a turning point in my prayer life.

Facing the impossible

As I was going through this time of major crises, I went to church one week with a very long face—I wanted people to know I was discouraged. At the end of Sabbath School, Muneer and Selma stopped and asked me why I looked sad. I explained that the situation had not gone away. I was still struggling with the four issues. They asked, "Did you pray about it?" In my heart, I knew that they were going to ask me this since we had already talked about the power of prayer the previous Sabbath.

"Of course I prayed about it," I said.

They went on to say, "But have you really prayed about it? Have you agonized over it? Do you believe that God is able to find a solution? What you describe to me sounds very difficult if not impossible. Yet think about it this way: You want God to change the policies of governments. You want God to change the policies of the army. You want Him to find thirty-two thousand dollars to help with your education and then find someone to guarantee you for ten thousand dollars. These seem like four impossibilities.

"You are kind of like the Israelites with the Red Sea in front and the Egyptian army behind, with no place to go. God is left with three options, all of which seem impossible. He can fly you over to where you want to go, kill the Egyptian army, or split the Red Sea."

Then they pressed the question, making it deeply personal, "Do you believe that God is able to do something in your life? Do you believe that He can change circumstances? Can He alter policies and history? Provide money? Can He change the hearts of people?"

I thought about it. They were right. It was going to take a miracle. The question now became, *Do I believe that God is able to perform that miracle? Do I have enough faith to believe that?*

Praying for a prison break

Muneer and Selma encouraged me to read stories in the Bible that illustrated the power of prayer. One day while reading the Bible, God opened my eyes to see the value of prayer. The story I read struck me and left a lasting impact on my life.

Immediately after Pentecost, Jesus' followers began sharing the gospel. The religious and political leaders felt threatened because of the dramatic increase in believers. Their efforts to combat their loss of influence included arrest and condemnation. Still the number of believers increased.

Eventually, King Herod arrested and beheaded James, the brother of John. When Herod saw the pleasure James's death brought to the religious leaders, he arrested Peter. While waiting for the day of Peter's execution, Herod tightened his security. Fourteen Roman soldiers were assigned to guard the entrance of the cell. Two other soldiers were chained to Peter; one was chained to his left wrist, one to his right.

The church prayed for Peter's deliverance, but hope faded as the date of his execution neared.

Finally, the night before Peter's execution arrived. As usual, the church continued to pray, and Peter slept peacefully in prison.

Suddenly an angel of the Lord appeared and a light shone in the cell. He struck Peter on the side and woke him up. "Quick, get up!" he said, and the chains fell off Peter's wrists.

Then the angel said to him, "Put on your clothes and sandals." And Peter did so. "Wrap your cloak around you and follow me," the angel told him. Peter followed him out of the prison, but he had no idea that what the angel was doing was really happening; he thought he was seeing a vision. They passed the first and second guards and came to the iron gate leading to the city. It opened for them by itself, and they went through it. When they had walked the length of one street, suddenly the angel left him (verses 7–10).

Once Peter realized that he was free, he went to the gathered believers. Rhoda, the servant girl, answered the door. When she recognized Peter's voice, she excitedly ran to tell the other believers, but they did not believe her: " 'You're out of your mind,' they told her. When she kept insisting that it was so, they said, 'It must be his angel.' But Peter kept on knocking, and when they opened the door and saw him, they were astonished" (verses 15, 16).

Even the first-century Christians questioned God's willingness to intervene in their circumstances. Still, they prayed; and God answered.

I learned that bold prayers honor God, and God honors bold prayers. "God isn't offended by your biggest dreams or boldest prayers. He is offended by anything less. If your prayers aren't impossible to you, they are insulting to God. Why? Because they don't require divine intervention. But ask God to part the Red Sea or make the sun stand still or float an iron axhead, and God is moved to omnipotent action."[1]

Whatever your request might be, do you regularly and diligently, every single day, bring it to God in prayer, trusting that He will intervene in your situation? If not, why not?

---

1. Mark Batterson, *The Circle Maker* (Grand Rapids, MI: Zondervan, 2011), 13.

Moving From Head to Heart

God's Power Released Through Prayer

And if we know that he hears us—whatever we ask—
we know that we have what we asked of him.

—1 John 5:15

In my head, I believed in God's omnipotence. I even talked about it. But this belief hadn't registered where it really counts—in my heart. Somewhere, deep down, I didn't believe He could do anything about the four problems I was facing: no money to pursue my education, no way of getting an exit visa from Iraq and an entry visa to the US, mandatory army service if I did not continue my education, and finding a sponsor to guarantee my return for $10,000. I had forgotten that prayer had resulted in the recognition of Middle East College by the Iraqi government and that prayer had saved my life from many dangers while I studied in Lebanon.

An assault on my lack of conviction

Frustrated with my lack of conviction, I planned a counterattack through studying stories in the Bible about God's power over nature. There were

- parting seas and rivers (Exodus 14; Joshua 3);
- extending the hours of daylight (Joshua 10:12–14, Isaiah 38:7, 8);

- sending manna, ravens with bread, and multiplying bread and fish (Exodus 16; 1 Kings 17:2–6; John 6:1–13); and
- calming a storm (Mark 4:35–41).

Bill Hybels writes about the dialogue between God and Moses over the way of providing water to the Israelites in the desert. "I imagine Moses saying, 'Yes, but what does a rock have to do with water? If we need water, let's look at the ground.'

"God answered, 'No, I don't want the people thinking you stumbled across an artesian well. I want you to know who has power over nature. I'm going to send you water right out of the side of that dry rock.' And He did."[1]

By studying these stories, I started to experience a new conviction. I became more certain of God's omnipotent power over His creation.

God can influence people

Next, because my needs required other people to step up and be willing to make changes on my behalf, I studied stories that demonstrate God's ability to influence human history, such as

- softening Pharaoh's heart (Exodus 11:1–8);
- strengthening David when others became discouraged (1 Samuel 17);
- encouraging Elijah (1 Kings 19:15); and
- calling Saul of Tarsus to become Paul the apostle (Acts 9:1–31).

One story that stood out from the New Testament was the story of Peter's denial in Caiaphas' courtyard. Jesus had been captured in the garden about midnight and brought to the religious and secular leaders; most of His followers escaped in fear. Peter did not do that. He followed at a distance and mingled with the crowd that entered the high priest's yard. Yet his thoughts grew darker. He figured that he and the other disciples would be next. He had to disguise himself to avoid his Master's fate.

Jesus knew what was about to happen. He knew both about the denial and Peter's potential for becoming one of the most courageous and influential leaders of the church (Acts 15:13–15; see also Matthew 16:18, 19). "Simon, Simon," Jesus told Peter that night, "Satan has asked to sift you as wheat. But I have prayed for you, Simon, that your faith may not fail. And when you have turned back, strengthen your brothers" (Luke 22:31, 32).

Peter did not understand those words at the time. He was too sad and broken to realize the promise in Jesus' words. He was going to undergo a transformation—but only by God's power. Only He can bring about this kind of change for those who trust Him.

My faith was growing. Like many others, first I became convinced of God's power over nature. Then I started to believe that He could change my own heart. These Bible texts were giving me the strength to say to myself that, no matter what others around me believed, God was real. Now, I was able to own personally the acknowledgement of God's powerful presence throughout history. There was no reason to believe that He had changed. He was still able to change the natural world and the human heart.

Time after time, the Bible tells us of God's ability to heal and save. He was able to give a child to ninety-one-year-old Sarah (Genesis 17:17–19; Romans 4:18–21). He can save three of His followers from a fiery furnace (Daniel 3:17). He could rescue Daniel from the lions' mouths (Daniel 6:20–22) and Paul and Silas from prison (Acts 16:16–29). He can provide for all our needs (2 Corinthians 9:8). He can save completely those who come to Him through Jesus (Hebrews 7:25). "He is able to do immeasureably more than all we ask or imagine" (Ephesians 3:20). Therefore, we should never be hesitant about asking God for anything—big or small.

If you want to grow beyond a fainthearted prayer life, you will need to own the conviction that God is all-powerful. You'll make a few wishes on your knees, but you won't be able to persevere in prayer until you know in your heart that God is able.

The God of the impossible

After I studied all these passages to the point of feeling this awesome power of God and experiencing it in my head and my heart—believing it is there and available to me—I started to pray over my four impossibilities: money for school, permission to leave the country, release from my army obligation, and someone to guarantee my return. I prayed for months, several hours every day—pleading with God to do the impossible. I spent many hours each day agonizing with God through prayer and fasting, claiming His promises. Also, for nine months, many people in the church prayed and fasted on my behalf.

Many things started to happen. Perhaps the most important thing was that I started to notice power in my life that I had never noticed before. I felt the presence of God: I felt Him everywhere. I felt His power surrounding me. My words were full of conviction. My faith was full of strength. I could say with absolute confidence that God was there, that He was close and available.

Problem solved

When I was at Middle East College, I met a student from the US, Mark, who promised to find a sponsor for me. After nine months of prayer, I received a letter from Walla Walla College stating that my finances for the first year were taken care of by an unknown individual. God has thousands of ways—not one, five, fifty, or one hundred—to provide for our needs, of which we know nothing. Some of them are unlikely, if not unbelievable. He sent food to Elijah through ravens, rained manna from heaven, brought forth water from rocks, and had an anonymous person pay for my schooling.

One day, a man from church came up to me and said, "I know you need someone to guarantee your return in order to leave the country. I'd like to do that." While I was praying, God was working on this man's heart. God has the power to soften hearts and influence them. Later on, I decided to stay in the United States. This man did not have to pay the government the guarantee because during Operation Desert Storm, the Iraqi Ministry of Education department building was bombed and all my records were lost.

Because this man stepped up to guarantee me, the United States granted me a student visa. As for the Iraqi government letting me leave, my request reached the desk of the prime minister, Saddam Hussein, who later on became the president. Iraq would have to make some changes to the law to allow me to leave. Thankfully, they made an exception and granted me the exit visa. God is in control of the destinies of the nations and of individuals. He set Peter, Daniel, and Moses free.

Because of the way God solved the problem of providing the financial assistance and visas, I was able to study abroad and not have to serve in the army.

God changed the policies of two governments and provided for my needs. I don't know how to explain it to you except to say that God is able. If He was able to split the Red Sea, save Israel, and drown the Egyptian army, then changing the laws of governments is no problem for Him.

It took faith in God's abilities to overcome my impossible situations.

Jesus said if you have faith as much as a mustard seed, you can say to this mountain, "Move," and this mountain will move and will be thrown to the bottom of the sea (Matthew 17:20).

Hang back no longer!

God, through Christ, has issued you a personal invitation to call on Him anytime. His door is always open. His Word tells us to "pray continually" (1 Thessalonians 5:17). This call to come to into Christ's presence is not limited based on how worthy you think you are. God's invitation is available to all, regardless of your life situation. If you are not a Christian yet, God says, "Come to me, all you who are weary and burdened, and I will give you rest. Take my yoke upon you and learn from me, for I am gentle and humble in heart, and you will find rest for your souls" (Matthew 11:28, 29).

If you are already God's child, you can pray about anything—big or small, possible or impossible. "Do not be anxious about anything, but in every situation, by prayer and petition, with thanksgiving, present your requests to God" (Philippians 4:6). You can pray wherever you are: "I want men everywhere to pray, lifting up holy hands without anger or disputing" (1 Timothy 2:8).

You don't need to be timid: "Let us then approach God's throne of grace with confidence, so that we may receive mercy and find grace to help us in our time of need" (Hebrews 4:16). You can be sure that your requests go directly to God: "I am not saying that I will ask the Father on your behalf. No, the Father himself loves you" (John 16:26, 27).

When you accept God's invitation, miracles begin to happen. "You do not have because you do not ask God" (James 4:2). You can't imagine the changes that will occur in your life—in your marriage, your family, your career, your ministry, and your witnessing. You must be convinced in the core of your being that God is willing, that He is able, and that He has invited you to come before His throne in prayer.

God is interested in your prayers because He is interested in you. Whatever matters to you is a priority for His attention. Nothing in the universe matters as much to Him as what is going on in your life today. "Are not two sparrows sold for a penny? Yet not one of them will fall to the ground outside your Father's care. And even the very hairs of your head are all numbered. So don't be afraid; you are worth more than many sparrows" (Matthew 10:29–31).

You don't have to pester Him to get His attention. You don't have to spend hours on your knees or flail yourself around or go without food to show Him you really mean business. He's your Father; He wants to hear what you have to say. In fact, He's waiting for you to call.

If one of my kids called me and said, "Dad, please, please, please, I beg you, I plead with you to listen to my request. Pretty please?" I'd say, "Time out. I don't like the underlying assumption here. You don't have to go through all those hoops. What in my life is more important than you? What gives me greater pleasure than meeting your needs? What can I do for you?"

"Come into my presence," God says. "Talk to Me. Share all your concerns. I'm keenly interested in you because I'm your Father. I'm able to help because all power in heaven and earth is mine. And I'm listening very closely for your voice."

---

1. Bill Hybels, *Too Busy Not to Pray* (Downer's Grove, IL: InterVarsity, 2008), 38.

The Descendants of Daniel, Shadrach, Meshach, and Abednego—Part 1

God's Strength in the Midst of Persecution

Let us hold fast the confession of our hope without wavering, for He who promised is faithful.
—Hebrews 10:23, NKJV

When I returned to Baghdad from Lebanon to wait for my visa to Walla Walla College, a story of national significance about the educational system and the Seventh-day Adventist Church took place.

I saw young men and women submitting their lives to God to the point of accepting a walk through the furnace of fire. They were a modern example of the three friends mentioned in the book of Daniel, a band of loyal believers who determined that they would rather die—be thrown into the furnace of fire—than to worship false gods.

The defining issue

There was only one difference between Daniel's band and the group I observed in Baghdad. The issue at the time of Daniel was the second commandment (Daniel 3; 6). The issue for the band I saw was the fourth commandment—the Sabbath commandment. In both cases, the defining issue was whether or not to be obedient to God.

In 1968, the Ba'th Party took over the government of Iraq. The Ba'th Party had a unique political structure. It was supposed to be a socialist party, but it was full of communists and leaned toward dictatorship. In fact, it even had some capitalist elements in it. Immediately after they had established themselves in power, they started a gradual process of nationalization of private industries, companies, corporations, and institutions. They started with oil companies and went on to heavy industries, such as steel, electric equipment, and so on.

The church knew that this nationalization would eventually be applied to the private institutions of education, which include universities, high schools, and elementary schools. The Seventh-day Adventists had an elementary school and an academy at that time in Iraq.

So the Adventist Church, on several occasions, prayed and asked God for an answer, for an exit, for a solution. The situation became serious when the government nationalized a university run by the Catholic Church, for if they took over that university, they would certainly nationalize other church-sponsored schools.

High stakes

The tension increased when some high-ranking officials in the government declared that the time was coming when every institution of education would be run according to the policies and regulations set by the Ministry of Education. That meant at least two major issues:

1. The indoctrination of the students by the doctrine and teaching of the Ba'th Party.
2. The implementation of a Sabbath test. Iraq is a Muslim country that has six work days. Friday is the day off because it is the holy day for the Muslims. The Sabbath is considered a workday and, therefore, even Adventist institutions would be required to have school on the Sabbath day.

The school year in Iraq starts in the middle of September and continues to the middle of June, similar to the system in America. In April 1975, before the start of the 1975–1976 school year, the government nationalized all the schools. They declared that all schools would run in harmony with the regulations and policies of the Ministry of Education. The 1975–1976 school year would be the first year within the new system. Any failure on the part of the students, teachers, or anyone else to carry out this change was a sign of disobedience to the government and would be punished under the penalty of the law.

From that time on, the Adventist church took the issue very seriously. The church started to pray every day and fast at least once a week. They asked God to solve this problem, to spread His mighty arms and deliver His people, to show His great interest, love, and concern for them.

They clung to the promise found in Psalm 44:3, "For by their own sword they did not possess the land, and their own arm did not save them, but Your right hand and Your arm and the light of Your presence, for You favored them" (NASB).

The preaching at that time was centered on the problem. The theme was "God is able to deliver us. Just trust in Him. God has an exit for us. He won't leave us alone." Two verses were repeated over and over from Isaiah, " 'No weapon forged against you will prevail, and you will refute every tongue that accuses you. This is the heritage of the servants of the LORD, and this is their vindication from me,' declares the LORD" (Isaiah 54:17). The second verse was Isaiah 63:7–9:

> I will tell of the kindnesses of the LORD,
>   the deeds for which he is to be praised,
>   according to all the LORD has done for us—
> yes, the many good things
>   he has done for Israel,
>   according to his compassion and many kindnesses.
> He said, "Surely they are my people,
>   children who will be true to me";
>   and so he became their Savior.
> In all their distress he too was distressed,
>   and the angel of his presence saved them.
> In his love and mercy he redeemed them;
>   he lifted them up and carried them
>   all the days of old.

Willful and deliberate absence

Time passed very slowly. The summer ended, and nothing happened. The government emphasized that everything was under control and that they had the full capacity to run every school according to their policies. Anyone who disobeyed would receive punishment.

When I talk about punishment, I am not talking about a fine of one hundred to five hundred dollars or about imprisonment of three to ten years. During the reign of the Ba'th Party, hundreds and thousands of people were hung and murdered everywhere, even in the main square of the capital city, Baghdad, for very trivial reasons or no reason at all.

The first week of the school year went fine. Everyone went to school every day, or so it seemed. About twenty-five students and teachers did not go to school on the Sabbath day, but it was very hard to notice them because schools in Iraq are very big, some having over a thousand students. (Our school was a small school of about two hundred students, but when the government nationalized it, they made it into a school of one thousand students.)

It was very difficult to notice twenty-five people missing, spread throughout the school, when you had a school of over a thousand people. (Even if you did notice them, it was very difficult to assume that all of these people had one purpose in mind: worship God on His holy day.) However, after a few weeks of missing school on the Sabbath day, the administration knew the reason and asked the teachers to stress the importance of coming to school on the Sabbath. It did not help. Daniel's band was still absent on the Sabbath day.

We ought to obey God rather than man

Finally, after several weeks of this repeated action of rebellion, the administration of the school gathered the Adventist teachers and students in one room and investigated the problem. They asked students from first to twelfth grade if their parents were forcing them not to come to school on the Sabbath day. The young worshipers said, "No, nobody is forcing us. We choose to go to church on the Sabbath day to worship God and to fellowship with His people. We love God, and we love to obey His commandments. The Sabbath is a day of worship, a day of communion with God, a day of rest, a day to receive a special blessing from God."

After spending a couple of hours with them, the administration said, "Well, we will forgive you this time. Just come to school next Sabbath."

Like Peter and the other apostles who replied, "We ought to obey God rather than men" (Acts 5:29, KJV), these descendants of Daniel, Shadrach,

Meshach, and Abednego chose to obey God rather than man. The following Sabbath, none of them showed up at school. This rebellion made the principal very angry, so he took the problem to the minister of education.

At the beginning, they sent letters to the students, the teachers, their families, and the church, threatening them to forget about the Sabbath and to be loyal to the government. When this did not work, the minister of education decided to make a drastic change and transfer the students and the teachers to different schools all over the country. His rationale was that if they were together, they would encourage each other, but if separated, the individual resolve would weaken. They would get discouraged, surrender, and forget about the whole issue.

Prayer circles

During this time of distress, I remembering meeting with my church at least two to three times every week to encircle the teachers and students with prayers of encouragement. We prayed that they would be faithful and stand firm and that God would solve this problem permanently. We prayed the prayer written by David while being persecuted by Saul, "Be strong and take heart, all you who hope in the LORD" (Psalm 31:24).

We studied the faith chapter in Hebrews 11 and read how different people such as Abraham, Moses, and Rahab stood faithful to God under difficult situations and trials. Men and women had to live in caves and even holes in the ground. Some were ridiculed, some stoned, some put in prison, and some killed by the sword for their faith. We affirmed that faith is confidence in God's grace so sure and certain that a man could stake his life on it a thousand times.

We kept reminding them that when we trust in the Lord, whatever difficulties or obstacles we might face, God will strengthen us. Those who hope in God have reasons to be of great courage.

Also, what kept those young people faithful was claiming their own promises from the Bible, such as, "The LORD is my strength and my defense; he has become my salvation. Shouts of joy and victory resound in the tents of the righteous: 'The LORD's right hand has done mighty things! The LORD's right hand is lifted high; the LORD's right hand has done mighty things!' " (Psalm 118:14–16).

The government was against them, as well as the educational system. So how did God solve this insurmountable problem?

The Descendants of Daniel, Shadrach, Meshach, and Abednego—Part 2

God's Testimony to the Nations

Surely the arm of the Lord is not too short to save,
nor his ear too dull to hear.

—Isaiah 59:1

We knew the time was coming when the students and teachers would be transferred across the country. We met one last time at the church to pray for them, ask God to deliver them, and remind them that God would be with them always.

The following day, the government shipped them all over the country. We had twenty-five people, each one sent to a different city in Iraq. Each person found foster parents to house him or her.

Faithfulness until the end

When the first Sabbath came, not one of them went to school. When this continued to happen, people started to ask them why they were missing school on the Sabbath. They started to share their faith with their foster parents, teachers, and the people in the communities where they were living.

They followed the command of Paul to walk in wisdom toward outsiders, making the best use of their time. Their speech was always gracious, seasoned with salt, so that they knew how to answer each person (Colossians 4:5, 6).

People all over Iraq learned about the importance of being faithful to God and keeping His Sabbath.

Because of the ministry of Daniel's three friends—Shadrach, Meshach and Abednego—who refused to bend a knee, the ancient world learned about Jehovah:

> Then Nebuchadnezzar said, "Praise be to the God of Shadrach, Meshach and Abednego, who has sent his angel and rescued his servants! They trusted in him and defied the king's command and were willing to give up their lives rather than serve or worship any god except their own God. Therefore I decree that the people of any nation or language who say anything against the God of Shadrach, Meshach and Abednego be cut into pieces and their houses be turned into piles of rubble, for no other god can save in this way" (Daniel 3:28, 29).

Modern-day Daniel and friends

As a result of the ministry of another band of loyal believers in the same land, the descendants of the Babylonian empire learned about the Sabbath and the Lord of the Sabbath.

Those faithful students and teachers took the message of obedience to God and His commandments to every school they attended. They rejoiced to speak about the rest we find in Christ on His holy day.

The issue came to the public, and thousands of people watched to see the outcome. Finally, when everything failed to force those students to go to school on the Sabbath day, the minister of education took the problem to the vice president of the country. When presented with the problem, he remembered a letter that was given to him by the president. The pastor of the Adventist church in Baghdad wrote this letter, which was an explanation of the Sabbath and an appeal for religious freedom.

The pastor's letter had been given to an Adventist female doctor who was taking care of the president's daughter while she was in the hospital with a severe case of pneumonia. The doctor gave the letter to the daughter, and the daughter gave it to her father.

Because of the many things he had to take care of, the president did not have the time to investigate the issue, so he authorized the vice president, Saddam Hussein, to take care of the letter and the problem. Because of excessive demands on his time, Saddam Hussein gave the letter to the minister of education, with his full support to any action the minister would take.

The minister of education took the letter and went to his office to study it. The letter consisted of twelve points that dealt with various issues, such as proving the Sabbath as the day of worship from the Bible and the Quran, the importance of obeying God and His commandments, and finally an appeal for religious freedom. After four hours of intensive study of these points, the minister called the pastor on the phone and made an appointment to meet with him the following morning.

Midnight cry

That night, the church met together, and a prayer went out to God crying and asking Him to intervene, to comfort His people, and to end their agony. In a situation such as this, you realize that your life depends on God.

The following day, the two men met together. The minister of education told the pastor that he had studied all of the points of the letter, looked at the issue very objectively, and had come to the conclusion that there was no justifiable reason for disobeying the law of the government. He stressed the point that those students and teachers should go to school on the Sabbath day. Anyone who would disobey would be under the punishment of the law, possibly even the death penalty.

Dark horizon

On our Christian journey, sometimes the horizon looks very dark. It looks like we are flooded with problems. We start asking, "God, where are You? Are You really interested in us? Do You really love and care for us?"

The descendants of Daniel, Shadrach, Meshach, and Abednego, along with the church, prayed and fasted for several months with no answer. They felt as if maybe God was not interested or did not hear them. As the church, students, and teachers were living the problem of keeping the Sabbath, every other problem came to the surface at the same time. People in that country hardly know the difference between Adventists and Jews because both of them keep the Sabbath. Many hate Jews, and, therefore, hate the Adventists.

In his discouragement, the pastor offered a short prayer in his heart and turned to the minister and said, "May I know how you viewed my points and answered them?" That question reopened the conversation between them, and the pastor explained each point and then answered each objection. At the end, there was dead silence.

Miracle worker

The minister of education broke the lengthy silence by saying, "I see your point." The result of that meeting, as an answer to the prayers offered by the faithful followers of Jehovah, was that they gave the Adventist students and teachers the choice to go back to their original school with the privilege of keeping the Sabbath. The schools continued to operate on Sabbath, but their teachers were required to tutor them and teach them what they missed on that day.

Also, no examinations were supposed to be given on Sabbath in the rooms where Adventists were found. In Iraq, we have a qualifying test to see if you qualify for college or not. For years, the Adventists had problems with that test because it always came on the Sabbath day. The government agreed to reschedule the time of this test so that it would not come on the Sabbath. This opened the door for Adventists to have the privilege of higher education in Iraq. The minister of education even publicly apologized. He said, "We caused this problem publicly. Therefore, I am going to go on television and apologize publicly to all of you." All of these privileges were still in effect until the 2003 invasion of Iraq.

The membership of the Adventist church in Iraq was about 200 members when this incident took place. Because of their faithfulness within a Muslim country, steeped in tradition, God gave the Adventists the freedom to carry out their religious practices.

The wisdom of God is infinitely higher than the wisdom of man. Sometimes we do not understand how He works, but let us be confident that He cares, loves, and watches over His children with everlasting mercy. Let us be confident that He will make everything, even the bad things, work for good for those who love Him (Romans 8:28). He sits on His throne on high. Nothing escapes His notice. He neither slumbers nor sleeps (Psalm 121:4), and His children are the great object of His interest (Zechariah 2:8).

Why wait?

God sometimes delays His answer and allows a time of testing for the following reasons:

1. *To teach us to depend on Him totally and completely.* All the doors were closed, and when all the doors are closed, the door of faith opens. Heaven wants us to know that without the help from above, we can't do anything, but with Christ's help, we can do all things (Philippians 4:13).

The government was against the Adventist students and teachers. People thought that they were crazy. Every door was sealed so that the only exit was to depend totally on God and to commit themselves to Him unconditionally.

Faith in God was the only way the friends of Daniel were able to go through the furnace of fire, and faith in God was the only way the modern descendants of Shadrach, Meshach, and Abednego were able to face the government. Faith is the best way to face the difficulties of life. Our problems might be different. They might be a loss of job or a financial crisis. They might be at home, at church, with friends, or on the job—but with Jesus, we can face them.

When everyone leaves, Jesus is there. Go to Him. He is willing to take you in His arms. The King of the whole universe is with you and on your side. What more do you need? We should never dwell on problems or consequences, but we should always dwell on Jesus. "Therefore, holy brothers and sisters, who share in the heavenly calling, fix your thoughts on Jesus, whom we acknowledge as our apostle and high priest" (Hebrews 3:1).

2. *To teach us to pray and study the Bible sincerely.* Crisis has the potential of deepening and strengthening our relationship with Christ, as it did for the church in Baghdad. I do not believe that God creates problems to help us grow, but I do believe that God uses life's problems to nurture our growth.

As I watched this story unfold, it strengthened my faith, encouraged my walk with God, and increased my boldness to witness for Him.

As Paul writes in Hebrews 12:1, 2: "Therefore, since we are surrounded by such a great cloud of witnesses, let us throw off everything that hinders and the sin that so easily entangles. And let us run with perseverance the race marked out for us, fixing our eyes on Jesus, the pioneer and perfecter of faith. For the joy set before him he endured the cross, scorning its shame, and sat down at the right hand of the throne of God."

The descendants of Daniel, Shadrach, Meshach and Abednego served as a great cloud of witnesses to me, the church in Baghdad, and the whole country.

3. *To strengthen our testimony and encourage us to share our faith with others.* Many people watched to see what would happen to the faithful teachers and students. Others wanted to take their stand for Christ, but they hesitated because they were afraid.

Becoming an Adventist in the Middle East may result in many difficulties. You might lose your friends and family, school or job, and receive the label "Jew," or a spy for Israel. At the time of Nebuchadnezzar, when people saw the God of Daniel, Shadrach, Meshach, and Abednego save them, many Babylonian people began to believe in Him. Years later, people again watched God perform this miracle of the Sabbath, and several people joined the church after witnessing God's provision for His people.

After I became an Adventist, several family members started to ask about and weigh the cost of following Jesus. Seeing how God worked in my life and others' helped them to take the step forward to accept Jesus and be fully devoted to Him.

God allowed this problem to get very complicated to strengthen the belief of His people in Him, to show them that He is still the ruler of the whole world. "For God is the King of all the earth; sing to him a psalm of praise" (Psalm 47:7).

4. *To spread the gospel message to unbelievers.* God's provision for His faithful teachers and students became a great, massive evangelistic crusade. Many people learned about Jehovah and His day of worship. Some heard it for the first time. For those who had heard it many times, it was a renewal of faith. It was a crusade to the outsiders and a revival to the insiders.

Whatever your problem is, remember that God is on your side. The psalmist writes, "The LORD is on my side; I will not fear. What can man do to me? The LORD is for me among those who help me; therefore I shall see my desire on those who hate me" (Psalm 118:6, 7, NKJV). You can face it and conquer it. Remember, you are not alone. Jesus says, "And surely I am with you always, to the very end of the age" (Matthew 28:20). Even when there is no room for God in your heart, remember that there is always room in the heart of God for you.

God wants people who take Him and His commandments seriously. He is interested in people who say, "I know I may lose my job, my family, and my friends, but what is important to me is to gain God." Jesus says to us, "Whoever wants to be my disciple must deny themselves and take up their cross and follow me" (Matthew 16:24).

This commitment and loyalty to God, this attitude of taking His law very seriously, does not come overnight, but it is the result of time spent with God. It is the result of a relationship and fellowship with Him. The only way for us not to bend a knee to the attractions of this world is to learn how to bend our knees to the King of this universe—God.

My Call to the Ministry

God's Confirmation of My Calling

"Before I formed you in the womb I knew you,
before you were born I set you apart;
I appointed you as a prophet to the nations."

—Jeremiah 1:5

I came to the United States from Baghdad, Iraq, to study engineering. At that time, I only knew a few words in English. When I arrived here, I cried because I could not communicate with people. Thankfully, God put a few people in my path that took an interest in me and started to teach me the language.

My desire in life was to start my own successful engineering firm. I wanted to have offices all over the world to allow me to buy all the toys my heart desired, to live in mansions, to drive fancy cars, and to travel all over the world. My focus in life was to acquire as much of this world as possible.

I did not forget the Lord. I still wanted to serve Him and advance His cause, but at that time, I was becoming more materialistic.

Everything will go up in smoke

One day, I was at Kretschmar Hall, the engineering building at Walla Walla College, with one of my classmates, working on a class project. In the middle of the project, we were stumped, so my friend started to read the Bible. Suddenly he looked at me, and I saw the excitement on his face. He told me he wanted me to read the text in 2 Peter that says:

> The Lord is not slow in keeping his promise, as some understand slowness. Instead he is patient with you, not wanting anyone to perish, but everyone to come to repentance. But the day of the Lord will come like a thief. The heavens will disappear with a roar; the elements will be destroyed by fire, and the earth and everything done in it will be laid bare. Since everything will be destroyed in this way, what kind of people ought you to be? You ought to live holy and godly lives as you look forward to the day of God and speed its coming. That day will bring about the destruction of the heavens by fire, and the elements will melt in the heat. But in keeping with his promise we are looking forward to a new heaven and a new earth, where righteousness dwells (2 Peter 3:9–13).

The words leaped off the pages of the Bible, straight into my heart and convinced me that everything will go up in smoke someday—except our relationship with God. It helped me to have a different perspective on life. It assisted me in rearranging my priorities. I started to focus on God again rather than material possessions. It brought me to the main purpose of my life—to serve God.

Discovery of my calling

A few weeks later, the men's dean asked me to give worship at a Friday night vespers. Afterward, someone came to me and told me that he really appreciated my talk. He then asked me if I had ever thought about going into the ministry. I told him I had thought about it from time to time—but never seriously.

"You need to," he said. "God is going to use you."

That evening, I couldn't go to sleep. I kept thinking about what this man had told me. I started again to examine the priorities of my life, the call and the content about the direction of my life. I spoke with one of the theology professors who dealt with counseling. He told me that a call to the ministry is a call from God, but often it is confirmed by the body of believers. He said that if people keep telling you to go into the ministry, you need to think about it very seriously.

I responded, "But how do they know that? I only preached once."

"You may want to make yourself available for preaching and see how people react," he suggested.

I left the counseling session thinking that if God wanted me to be a pastor, He had to bring the invitations to me. I was not going to pursue the calling—the invitation must be from Him. It wasn't long before many invitations started to come! Many people started to affirm my call to the ministry. That was in spite of my lack of knowledge of the English language, with poor pronunciation, syntax, grammar, and a limited vocabulary. Somehow people were blessed and came to me to tell me to go into the ministry.

After that, I took a few days to fast and pray—wrestling with the Bible and God. I read about the calls of other people. A few months later, I decided God really did want me to become a pastor. In order to fulfill the requirement of the visa I came on, I still had to study engineering, so I decided to do a double major. In 1980, I graduated from Walla Walla College with a degree in engineering and a degree in theology.

At that time, conferences were not hiring foreigners as pastors, so I was at a disadvantage. In December of every year, there was a banquet for all the graduating theology students and conference presidents, secretaries, and ministerial directors to help them get to know us and see if we would be a good fit for any of their churches.

My great disappointment

In December 1979, before my graduation the following summer, the twenty-six graduating theology students met with the officers of the conferences of the Northwest. This process took place over the course of three days. On the first day, Sunday night, there was a banquet. On the second day, in the morning, each one of us had five minutes to share why and how God called us into the ministry. On Monday afternoon, continuing through Tuesday, each of the students interviewed with the officers of the five conferences in the Northwest.

The calls started to come to the graduating theology majors in January 1980 and continued all the way to the end of February. However, no call came to me. In fact, one of the conference presidents told me I would never get a job in the ministry. I did not know the language well enough and did not understand the culture or people. He reminded me that I came from a place ten thousand miles away. His last words to me were, "Just forget about it. You will never make it."

I thought that maybe he was right. I interviewed for an engineering job. After half an hour, I told the interviewer, "I am wasting your time. I really want to be a pastor." Then a friend of mine called his father, who worked in Kuwait. They offered me a good-paying engineering job in their company, but I declined.

Another friend encouraged me and told me that God had a wonderful plan for my life. He claimed the promise of Jeremiah 29:11–13 for me: " 'For I know the plans I have for you,' declares the LORD, 'plans to prosper you and not to harm you, plans to give you hope and a future. Then you will call on me and come and pray to me, and I will listen to you. You will seek me and find me when you seek me with all your heart.' " He told me that God had a purpose in mind for me. It did not matter what the conference president said. The call would ultimately come from God.

The confirmation of my calling

Two days before graduation in June, six months after everyone else had received a call; I got the call to the Upper Columbia Conference. In the course of the interview with the ministerial director of the conference, he said to me, "We are willing to take a chance on you. I know you don't know the language or culture well, but when you went with ten students in 1978 to do Bible work in Chicago, the people there were very impressed with the quality of work you did. You even baptized some as a result. We received many positive reviews of your preaching. Therefore, we are going to extend a call to you to come pastor in our conference. We are going to send you to Spokane Valley to work with Russell Burrill."

I went to Spokane Valley on July 1, 1980. On my first Sabbath, as they introduced me to the congregation, they asked me to read the scripture text. It was 1 Timothy 1:17: "Now to the King eternal, immortal, invisible, the only God, be honor and glory for ever and ever. Amen."

I tried to speak with confidence, hoping to impress the church. But when I finished reading the text, an uproar of laughter came over the congregation. I did not know why. When I sat down and asked Russell Burrill what happened, he said to me, "Do not talk to me about it right now." He didn't want to laugh and wanted to be ready for his sermon.

Later on, he explained to me that rather than reading "To the King eternal, immortal, invisible," I had read, "To the King eternal, immoral, invisible."

When I discovered what I did, I grew very discouraged. On my first day, I blew it. I felt that I would never make it as a pastor. The words of the conference president came back to haunt me, "You are not equipped to pastor here."

My encouragers

Thankfully, someone came to me and said, "Maybe you are discouraged today because of what happened to you. I want you to remember, when Joshua took the helm of leadership from Moses, he was inexperienced and felt inadequate to lead the people of Israel. But God had these words for him, which also apply to you, 'Have I not commanded you? Be strong and of good courage; do not be afraid, nor be dismayed, for the LORD your God is with you wherever you go' [Joshua 1:9, NKJV]." The focus of what God said to Joshua is that God's presence would make up for all of the weaknesses and failures of Joshua. That is exactly what God does for us.

Another caring individual came to me and said, "When God is with us, there is no need to worry about failure. Jeremiah, when he was called as a youth, felt inexperienced and unqualified. 'But the LORD said to me, "Do not say, 'I am too young.' You must go to everyone I send you to and say whatever I command you. Do not be afraid of them, for I am with you and will rescue you," declares the LORD' [Jeremiah 1:7, 8]."

Much like Jeremiah, I was young and inexperienced when I went to my first church in July 1980. I spent almost two wonderful years pastoring a great church and working alongside a great pastor before going to the seminary.

The love of my life

During my fourth year of college, Walla Walla had the students try a computer dating program to match potential dates. I did not trust the matching system, so I decided to ask my friend Denise to answer the questions to match mine. As I expected, it did not work. We were not matched as potential dates. However, I asked her out anyway, and we went to a local pizza place. We recognized the chemistry between us, so we started dating. After dating for almost two years, Denise and I married during my first year of pastoral work. We have been married now for more than thirty-five years, and the Lord has blessed us with two wonderful children, Jason and Stephanie.

Looking back

Now, as I look back at my life, I realize that God was always with me. He gave me my call to the ministry in spite of the strikes against me. He gave me great churches to pastor. Under God's leadership and influence, and through the power of prayer, each church grew significantly. He made up for my failures. He has continued to be with me and bless me with success during my more than thirty-seven years of ministry.

God's presence makes up for our weaknesses, imperfections, fears, and inadequacies. His presence is our ultimate resource in the battle against the difficulties of life. I learned that living in awareness of God's presence means I do not have to worry about being overcome by failure. God has a plan and purpose for each one of us. It is through living in His presence that we can become confident, knowing that He is preparing the way.

The Surprise of My Life

God's Favor Over Me

> *Trust in the Lord with all your heart*
> *and lean not on your own understanding;*
> *in all your ways submit to him,*
> *and he will make your paths straight.*
> —Proverbs 3:5, 6

I came to United States knowing virtually none of the language, with half a dollar in my pocket. I spent four years dealing with language problems and financial difficulties. However, the Lord was always with me and helped me to finish my college education with two degrees in theology and engineering.

The Lord provided financially for me. The first year at Walla Walla College, an anonymous donor paid my entire tuition. After that, I worked during the summers as a colporteur and worked during the school year as a reader for a theology professor. I received help from others to pay for part of my education. I graduated college with only a $5,000 debt and paid it off during my first year pastoring.

I have experienced to the fullest what Paul says in Philippians 4:19, "My God will meet all your needs according to the riches of his glory in Christ Jesus." Since I have been blessed and received help financially while in school,

I try to support students with their tuition so that they can also have the benefit of Christian education.

My strong call to the ministry led me to pastor in Spokane Valley for a year and a half. Then I went to the seminary for three years, came back, and pastored in the Upper Columbia Conference until 2000. That year, I left to teach at the Seventh-day Adventist Theological Seminary in Michigan, and I have been here for the past seventeen years.

The ultimate surprise

While living in the United States since 1976, I have had limited contact with my family. In the beginning, contact was more frequent, but because of the wars, sometimes communications were completely shut down. Even when we were in contact, we had to be extremely careful with what we said because the Iraqi government bugged all telephones. Officials screened calls to make sure nothing was said or planned against the government of Iraq. Not only that, but the wars destroyed most of the communication infrastructure. Especially after Operation Iraqi Freedom in 2003, we did not have any communication for a long time.

In March 2003, the last war between Iraq and the United States started over weapons of mass destruction. Two years after the war started, my female cousin Suhelah, who came to the United States for advanced medical training, decided to return to Iraq to see how our family was doing. Being a female, she felt relatively safe at that time. She spent three months in Iraq. When she came back, I went to see her in Detroit, where she lives. She said to me, "Sit down. You are never going to believe what I am going to tell you. Your mom is praying and thanking the Lord for the Sabbath every day."

I said, "That does not make any sense. My mom kicked me out of my home because I started to keep the Sabbath."

She continued, "Your mom is praising the Lord for your faithfulness every day."

"Why?" I asked. "My mom was upset with me."

Suhelah told me my mom said, "I know that the Lord was guiding my son to do what he did. I am very glad that we beat him up, spit on him, and kicked him out of the home. If it wasn't for that, he never would have left the country and avoided enlisting in the army. He is alive today because of what we did." My cousin continued to say that my mother was studying the

Bible with my cousin Basher, the Adventist pastor, and now attended the Adventist church on a regular basis.

Suhelah explained to me that the reason my mom said I am alive today was because, shortly after I left Iraq in 1976 and came to the United States, Iraq started a war with its neighbor Iran over a water dispute. That war lasted for ten years, and approximately one million people, mostly from my age-group, died during this war. As soon as that war ended, Iraq invaded its neighbor Kuwait. This led to the first war with the United States in 1990–1991, called Operation Desert Shield and Operation Desert Storm. Then there was a minor war in 1998 between the two countries called Operation Desert Fox. Finally, there was a larger conflict in 2003, Operation Iraqi Freedom.

During that time, another million Iraqi people were killed. My mother continually said, "I thank God every day that my son is alive and does not have to go through all these problems. The Lord was guiding him to keep the Sabbath."

A few months after my cousin came back from Iraq, my mom was baptized into the Adventist Church. She did not tell me that she was thinking about becoming an Adventist until her baptism in 2005 because she wanted to surprise me.

Three months after her baptism, she passed away. My mom was diabetic, and there was no adequate medication available for her. Suhelah told me my mom died citing one of her favorite psalms:

Bless the LORD, O my soul;
And all that is within me, bless His holy name!
Bless the LORD, O my soul,
And forget not all His benefits:
Who forgives all your iniquities,
Who heals all your diseases,
Who redeems your life from destruction,
Who crowns you with lovingkindness and tender mercies,
Who satisfies your mouth with good things,
So that your youth is renewed like the eagle's.

. . . .

He has not dealt with us according to our sins,
Nor punished us according to our iniquities.

For as the heavens are high above the earth,
So great is His mercy toward those who fear Him;
As far as the east is from the west,
So far has He removed our transgressions from us.
As a father pities his children,
So the Lord pities those who fear Him.
For He knows our frame;
He remembers that we are dust (Psalm 103:1–14, NKJV).

I wish I had been there to witness her baptism, but I am looking forward to seeing her one day in heaven.

My father and I reconciled before I came to the United States. He even came to the airport to wish me farewell. He gradually accepted me as his son again and occasionally called to tell me he loved me and was proud of me. He never became an Adventist, as he never showed much interest in spirituality, although born in the Orthodox Church. My father passed away months after my mom.

My two brothers lived under dire conditions because of the war and the situation in Iraq. I have been praying for both of my brothers' safety and for their opportunity to leave the country and come to the United States. The Lord answered one of my prayers. In September 2015, I met one of my brothers, Wadallah, and his family at the airport in Kalamazoo, Michigan, seeing him for the first time in thirty-eight years.

Wadallah was granted permanent refugee status to settle in this country. I am still praying for my other brother, Janan, and his family to come here.

Forty years in the making

This story has been in the making for more than forty years, but I did not know until thirty years into it that I am alive today because of my faithfulness to God. I have experienced and seen with my own eyes that "all things God works for the good of those who love him, who have been called according to his purpose" (Romans 8:28).

When God makes all things work together for good, He is showing His favor toward us. "You have granted me life and favor, and Your care has preserved my spirit" (Job 10:12, NKJV).

Despite the rejection, persecution, and trials we experience, God's favor will bring joy to our lives. "For His anger is but for a moment, His favor is for life; weeping may endure for a night, but joy comes in the morning" (Psalm 30:5, NKJV). The ultimate favor God gives us is the Holy Spirit to dwell in us. He is what gives us hope, courage, and endurance.

A random walk one Friday afternoon changed the trajectory of my life and that of my family forever. Looking back, I believe God was guiding me to the Adventist church so that I could see the movie about Jesus. This was a divine appointment. Falling in love with Him became the defining moment in my life and in the lives of so many other people.

God is in charge of our lives. There is no reason for us to be afraid. He always leads, guides, and makes things to work for good for us. Ellen G. White writes, "We have nothing to fear for the future, except as we shall forget the way the Lord has led us, and His teaching in our past history."[1]

---

1. Ellen G. White, *Life Sketches* (Nampa, ID: Pacific Press®, 2002), 196.

Jesus, the Savior of My Life

God's Love and Lordship in My Life

But God demonstrates his own love for us in this:
While we were still sinners, Christ died for us.
—Romans 5:8

My experience with God has taught me many lessons about the way God has been leading and guiding in my life. The following three chapters are dedicated to those lessons.

Falling in love with Jesus

First, I learned Jesus loves me. The minute I saw Jesus on that movie screen forty years ago and saw what He did for me, I fell in love with Him. Although I have sinned and fallen short of the glory of God, Christ still loves and accepts me. He took my place and died for me, and He was resurrected on my behalf. "For all have sinned and fall short of the glory of God, and all are justified freely by his grace through the redemption that came by Christ Jesus" (Romans 3:23, 24).

I devoted the rest of my life to learning more about Jesus and His love. It motivated me to study the Bible with Pastor Doss and on my own. It caused me to look at everything—doctrines, teachings, and sermons—in the context of Jesus' love. His love drove me to feel close to Him. I want to live in the awareness of His loving presence. Jesus is the heart of Christianity, the heart of the church, the heart of the Bible, and the King of my heart.

Zephaniah 3:17 reiterates the personal love the King of our hearts has for each of us: "The Lord your God is with you, the Mighty Warrior who saves. He will take great delight in you; in his love he will no longer rebuke you, but will rejoice over you with singing."

As God has shown His love for me, I show my love for God in many different ways. I carve out time from my busy schedule to spend times of sweet fellowship with God, listening and responding to what He wants to say to me. In spite of His busy schedule of teaching, healing, and traveling, Jesus always took the time to be with His heavenly Father. "Immediately Jesus made the disciples get into the boat and go on ahead of him to the other side, while he dismissed the crowd. After he had dismissed them, he went up on a mountainside by himself to pray" (Matthew 14:22, 23).

I also show my love to God by recognizing that everything belongs to Him, and the most important thing I have to give is myself. "Therefore, I urge you, brothers and sisters, in view of God's mercy, to offer your bodies as a living sacrifice, holy and pleasing to God—this is your true and proper worship" (Romans 12:1). As we give of ourselves, we must give everything to Him: our gifts, our talents, and our resources. "The earth is the Lord's, and everything in it, the world, and all who live in it" (Psalm 24:1).

As I love God, I think of how I can be of service to the people God has placed around me. "God is not unjust; he will not forget your work and the love you have shown him as you have helped his people and continue to help them" (Hebrews 6:10).

We can feel God's love for us through His presence through the good times and the bad times. Ellen G. White wrote: "Since Jesus came to dwell with us, we know that God is acquainted with our trials, and sympathizes with our griefs. Every son and daughter of Adam may understand that our Creator is the friend of sinners. For in every doctrine of grace, every promise of joy, every deed of love, every divine attraction presented in the Savior's life on earth, we see 'God with us.'"[1]

Living by the Lordship of Jesus Christ

Second, I learned to accept and live by the Lordship of Jesus Christ. Each one of us is confronted with some kind of Lordship test: obedience, Sabbath, tithing, faithfulness, and so on. When we face these tests, our tendency is to focus on the problems and the challenges. However, Scripture teaches us to fasten our eyes on Jesus, the Author and Perfecter of our faith (Hebrews 12:2). The heart of the Lordship issue is trust. God is asking each one of us, "Who is number one in your life? Do you trust Me?" When the compass of your heart moves, does it move toward Jesus?

I deeply understand how tough it can be to surrender everything to Jesus. I struggled with this personally for many years. What we need to understand is what's behind our lack of surrender. Why is it that we're afraid? In my experience, we fear surrendering to God because, deep down, we don't believe that He is good. In other words, I will surrender to someone that I know has my best interest in mind. The issue is not surrender, the issue is unbelief.

One of the things that helped me to surrender fully was to study the attributes of God. God is good, gracious, merciful, long-suffering, faithful, omnipresent (present all the time), eternal, holy, just, loving, righteous, sovereign, and powerful (Exodus 34:6, 7; Psalm 25:8; Psalms 95–99; James 1:17). He is great and full of goodness at the same time.

The other thing that really helped me was reading the Gospel of John. There are eight miracles that Jesus performed that show His power over everything—disease, nature, distance, and even death. If Jesus did all of this, He could do the same thing for me:

- He turned the water into wine (John 2:1–12). Jesus turned their sadness into gladness.
- He healed the son of the royal official (nobleman [KJV, NKJV]) (John 4:46–54). Jesus restored the son from disease to health.
- He healed the man who was crippled for thirty-eight years at the pool of Bethesda (John 5:1–15). Jesus turned his lifelong paralysis into instant activity.
- He fed the five thousand (John 6:1–13). Jesus turned their hunger into full satisfaction.
- He calmed the storm and walked on the water (John 6:16–20). Jesus turned nature's agitation into peace.
- He healed the blind man (John 9:1–12). Jesus turned his darkness into light.
- He raised Lazarus from the dead (John 11:38–44). Jesus brought

the dead man, Lazarus, back to life. Only an all-powerful God can do that.

- He provided a second great catch of fish (John 21:1–6). Jesus turned the disciples' failure into abundant success.

Jesus urges us in Scripture to surrender ourselves to Him. "Surrender yourself to the LORD, and wait patiently for him" (Psalm 37:7, GW). This will manifest itself in different ways. Surrender includes

- answering God's call without question,
- waiting on Him with expectant faith, and
- trusting Him regardless of outside circumstances.

You have experienced full surrender when you no longer feel the need to control your own life. Rather than struggling, you simply rest in the knowledge that *God is able.*

For many, the most difficult thing to surrender is our will. We might think, "I want to live for God, but I at least want partial control over my circumstances."

Jesus provides us with the clearest example of surrender. His struggle in Gethsemane ended with this prayer of surrender, " 'Abba, Father, . . . everything is possible for you. Take this cup from me. Yet not what I will, but what you will' " (Mark 14:36). In praying this, Jesus surrendered Himself to His Father's will.

Complete surrender recognizes that God uses every situation to work "for the good of those who love him, who have been called according to his purpose" (Romans 8:28). However, choosing complete surrender is difficult. We like to be in control, and surrender removes that possibility. In order to reach complete surrender, self must be crucified with Christ—and we must allow Christ to live in and through us (see Galatians 2:20).

Surrender cannot be halfway. Just as we would not give our spouse 50 percent of our loyalty, we cannot give God partial commitment either. God loves us so much and deserves all of our devotion.

When we look back at the struggle we had to surrender, we see how it was the best thing that ever happened to us. I have personally experienced this. As I reflect upon my life, I remember how hard it was for me to surrender, thinking of all the problems I would encounter. After I surrendered, God made all of those problems work for good for my family and me. It was the best thing that ever happened to me.

---

1. Ellen G. White, *The Desire of Ages* (Nampa, ID: Pacific Press®, 2002), 24.

Jesus, the King of My Heart

God's Centrality in My Life

And let us run with perseverance the race marked out for us, fixing our eyes on Jesus, the pioneer and perfecter of faith. For the joy set before him he endured the cross, scorning its shame, and sat down at the right hand of the throne of God.

—Hebrews 12:2

Focus on Jesus Christ

Third, I learned to focus on Jesus Christ. We often focus on our problems, difficulties, and challenges. For many years in my life, I believed in a very small God. Notwithstanding, the God we worship is a great God who can do the impossible, such as move mountains and kill giants. He is the Creator that is in control of the entire universe, as well as your own little world. How big is your God?

For years, I postponed my decision to follow Jesus, fearing the consequences. Everything I was afraid would happen, happened. But the great and awesome God we serve made all things work for good for His glory and for my own benefit, as well as my family's benefit.

There are several stories in the Bible telling us that our God is the God of the impossible. One day, God came to a woman who was barren all of her life. She was ninety years old, and her husband was one hundred years old.

God said to her, "I will give you a child." Sarah laughed because she thought it was a joke. After all, she was more a candidate for the nursing home—not the maternity ward! But God gave her the child anyway (Genesis 17:17; 18:10–14).

Centuries later, the angel Gabriel came to a virgin and said to her, "You will conceive and give birth to a son, and you are to call him Jesus" (Luke 1:31). Mary believed him and had the privilege of becoming the mother of Jesus Christ.

One day, God showed a young boy that if he trusted in Him, he could defeat a giant, and David did (1 Samuel 17).

Today, He comes to you and to me and says if we have faith as small as a mustard seed, we can move mountains, conquer the impossible, and overcome obstacles (Matthew 17:20). Whatever mountain you are facing in your life, whether financial, marital, or health-related, God is bigger than that. Our God is the God of the impossible.

Nothing is too difficult for Him—a reality that Scripture testifies to again and again. The entire weight of the Scriptures is based on faith in a God who can do all things.

> Ah, Sovereign LORD, You have made the heavens and the earth by your great power and outstretched arm. Nothing is too hard for you. . . . You performed signs and wonders in Egypt and have continued them to this day, in Israel and among all mankind, and have gained the renown that is still yours. You brought your people Israel out of Egypt with signs and wonders, by a mighty hand and an outstretched arm and with great terror (Jeremiah 32:17–21).

Jesus confirms that God can do all things by saying, "With man this is impossible, but not with God; all things are possible with God" (Mark 10:27; see also Matthew 19:26 and Luke 18:27).

When people believe in the power of God, He rewards them with His rich and abundant blessings. The Lord is still almighty. Our faith is based on His unchanging nature, His abundant power, and His faithful promises.

When I was at Middle East College, I spoke with somebody about the possibility of going to Walla Walla College to study engineering. He said, "Don't even think about it. It's impossible to do that."

"Why is it impossible?" I asked.

"First, you don't know the language," he replied. "Second, you don't have money. And these are just the minor problems!"

So I asked him, "What is the major problem?"

He replied, "The United States of America is not accepting anyone from Iraq, and Iraq is not giving permission for anyone to leave the country and go to the United States. This situation is so impossible that it was easier for Moses to take the children of Israel out of Egypt and into the Promised Land than for you to go from Iraq to study in the United States." What a man of encouragement he was!

This man forgot the main point of the Exodus story. It wasn't Moses who took them to the Promised Land. It was the all-powerful God. This same God is available to us today to take care of any problem we have. He specializes in doing the impossible, and that is exactly what He did. Miraculously, as a result of my prayers and the prayers of the church in Iraq, the United States gave me the visa and the prime minister, Saddam Hussein, signed my passport so that I could leave the country and come here to study. God made an evil dictator sign my passport, and I know that the same God can and will do great miracles in the lives of all of us.

Focus on the privilege and power of prayer

Fourth, I learned about the privilege and the power of prayer. Jesus has promised that when we pray, God will be with us. "When you pray, go to your room and close the door. Pray privately to your Father who is with you. Your Father sees what you do in private. He will reward you" (Matthew 6:6, GW). David, with confidence, assures us that the Lord is with us when we pray and call on Him: "The LORD is near to all who call on him, to all who call on him in truth" (Psalm 145:18; see also Deuteronomy 4:7). This is God's desire. He wants you to draw near to Him. God is closer than we think. He is never farther than a prayer away. Every moment, when we pray, He hears.

Prayer allows us to experience the presence of God as we earnestly seek Him. "'Then you will call on me and come and pray to me, and I will listen to you. You will seek me and find me when you seek me with all your heart. I will be found by you,' declares the LORD," (Jeremiah 29:12–14). God is all around you. He is trying to talk to you, trying to make a difference in your life. God is seeking to show Himself to you in your day-to-day routine. The only way that you can see Him, the only way you can realize His presence, is to set your mind and your heart to seek Him. The only way to find something is to look for it. Acknowledge His presence and talk to Him about all the issues in your life. Determine to find God's presence and to live God's will. Don't allow anything to distract you.

The psalmist expounds upon the idea of earnestly seeking God by declaring, "You, God, are my God, earnestly I seek you; I thirst for you, my whole being longs for you, in a dry and parched land where there is no water" (Psalm 63:1). The dry lands of abandonment, confusion, and suffering are transformed when we seek and thirst for God. His presence makes all the difference. It gives us confidence, peace, and hope.

Ellen G. White expounds upon prayer by saying it is the equivalent of living in the sunshine of His presence:

It is our privilege to open our hearts, and let the sunshine of Christ's presence in. My brother, my sister, face the light. Come into actual, personal contact with Christ, that you may exert an influence that is uplifting and reviving. Let your faith be strong and pure and steadfast. Let gratitude to God fill your hearts. When you rise in the morning, kneel at your bedside, and ask God to give you strength to fulfill the duties of the day, and to meet its temptations. Ask Him to help you to bring into your work Christ's sweetness of character. Ask Him to help you to speak words that will inspire those around you with hope and courage, and draw you nearer to the Savior.[1]

Muneer and Selma taught me a lot about meaningful prayer and living a life full of the presence of God. Ellen G. White writes, "Unceasing prayer is the unbroken union of the soul with God."[2] They taught me that prayer is not about a set time but a continual connection with God that happens at any time of the day or night. It is the opening of the heart to Jesus as to our best friend. We can be praying as we are studying, walking, cooking, or driving. "Rejoice always, pray without ceasing, in everything give thanks; for this is the will of God in Christ Jesus for you" (1 Thessalonians 5:16–18, NKJV).

One of their favorite quotations that they shared with me was, "Cultivate the habit of talking with the Savior when you are alone, when you are walking, and when you are busy with your daily labor. Let the heart be continually uplifted in silent petition for help, for light, for strength, and for knowledge. Let every breath be a prayer."[3]

Prayer is also about experiencing the power of God. "He shall call upon me, and I will answer him; I will be with him in trouble, I will deliver him and honor him" (Psalm 91:15). Prayer opened the door for the state recognition of Middle East College. The church tried for forty years to get the college to be recognized, and they failed. But when they prayed, God did it. Prayer was how I got the visa from the United States. Prayer even made Saddam Hussein sign my passport in October 1976 so I could leave Iraq and go to Walla Walla College. Prayer can only explain this miracle. Prayer provided a sponsor for me in the United States who also paid for part of my school bill. Prayer provided for all of my needs. Prayer made Basher's machine produce double the amount of fertilizer in five days than it did in six days. My prayers on behalf of my family were answered, and many of them came to know Jesus, including my two brothers and my mom. Prayer can change your life, solve your problems, bring Jesus closer to you, and help you feel His power and presence.

God loves us and wants to be with each of us individually. When we fail to pray and are out of fellowship with God, not only are we missing Him, but He is missing us. If I fall out of relationship with God, there is a Joseph Kidder–shaped hole in His heart. If you fall out of relationship with Him, there is a *you*-shaped hole in His heart that cannot be filled by any other person. Each one of us is uniquely special and loved by Him. God delights in you; you are precious in His sight.

---

1. Ellen G. White, *Sons and Daughters of God* (Hagerstown, MD: Review and Herald®, 2003), 199.

2. White, *Steps to Christ*, 98.

3. Ellen G. White, *The Ministry of Healing* (Nampa, ID: Pacific Press®, 2003), 510, 511.

Jesus, the Hope of My Future

God's Faithfulness in My Life

The LORD is good to those who wait for Him,
to the soul who seeks Him.
—Lamentations 3:25, NKJV

Embracing the promises

Fifth, I learned about the importance of reading the Bible every day. Muneer and Selma taught me to start every day with a meaningful devotion time, which included reading Scripture, praying, singing, and thinking about a mission activity to do for the day. One of the important reasons to start the day reading Scripture is so the Word of God will be our guide for that day. "Your word is a lamp for my feet, a light on my path" (Psalm 119:105). We need to have God's thoughts and ideas with us the whole day so we can meditate upon them and receive wisdom and insight to make the right decisions throughout the day. The study of the Bible will give strength to the intellect. Says the psalmist, "The unfolding of your words gives light; it gives understanding to the simple" (Psalm 119:130).

We also ended every day with having a short devotional where we read Scripture, prayed, and sang so we could go to bed with thoughts of God on our minds. Later on, they encouraged me to take the time to read Scripture and pray on my own. During that time, I came to appreciate the Word of God and fall more in love with Jesus as a result of reading it. "As we meditate upon the perfections of the Savior, we shall desire to be wholly transformed and renewed in the image of His purity. There will be a hungering and thirsting of soul to become like Him whom we adore. The more our thoughts are upon Christ, the more we shall speak of Him to others and represent Him to the world."[1]

My daily devotional time was a blessing in my life, and I am determined to continue it for the rest of my life. I never want to start a day without taking the time to be in the presence of Jesus.

Fill the whole heart with the words of God. They are the living water, quenching your burning thirst. They are the living bread from heaven. Jesus declares, "Except ye eat the flesh of the Son of man, and drink His blood, ye have no life in you." And He explains Himself by saying, "The words that I speak unto you, they are spirit, and they are life." John 6:53, 63. Our bodies are built up from what we eat and drink; and as in the natural economy, so in the spiritual economy: it is what we meditate upon that will give tone and strength to our spiritual nature.[2]

As I have been reading Scripture, I have found joy and comfort in the promises of God. There are 5,467 promises, according to Bible Gateway,[3] to meet every need. I do not think I could have made it without these promises. Reading them and claiming them are two different things. Learn the promises. Memorize them. Live by them. Experience them.

One of the promises we repeated and claimed every day was Romans 8:28: "And we know that in all things God works for the good of those who love him, who have been called according to his purpose."

Here is another promise that we claimed repeatedly: "In my distress I called to the Lord; I cried to my God for help. From his temple he heard my voice; my cry came before him, into his ears" (Psalm 18:6). God also heard my cries and answered them in a very powerful way. My trouble led to the conversion of many members of my family.

Another promise that meant so much to me is found in 2 Timothy 4:18: "The Lord will rescue me from every evil attack and will bring me safely to his heavenly kingdom. To him be glory for ever and ever. Amen." When we have a broader perspective on life and look at the big picture, we see that the Lord is working behind the scenes on behalf of those who follow and are faithful and obedient to Him. I faced many difficulties, but God turned them around and made them to be a blessing for others and myself.

Another claimed promise declares, "The LORD will keep you from all harm—he will watch over your life" (Psalm 121:7). This was fulfilled in my life in Beirut, Lebanon, during the civil war. Many times, the Lord rescued me from all the evil that was around me. He was my hiding place. "You are my hiding place; you will protect me from trouble and surround me with songs of deliverance" (Psalm 32:7).

In a time when I felt everything was against me, this promise was very precious because Jesus had become my hiding place. I could rest in Him and forget about all the troubles I was facing.

Eagerly waiting in anticipation
Sixth, I also learned the discipline of patience and timing. "Wait for the LORD; be strong and take heart and wait for the LORD" (Psalm 27:14). Scholars are not in agreement as to when David penned this psalm, whether after a crisis or at the end of his life. Regardless, it is very expressive of the sincere affections that gracious souls have for God at all times, especially in times of trouble.

It's hard for us to wait on the Lord. We want instant answers from Him. Modern culture has conditioned us to expect instant gratification, instant answers, and instant payoff. I have experienced many instances of waiting on the Lord. One of the most difficult ones was waiting for nine months for an exit visa from Iraq and an entry visa from the United States. Every day during that time, I prayed, but I did not know what the answer was going to be. At times, I even doubted that God would intervene. This is where the element of waiting and trusting in God becomes important.

Sometimes the seeds that God places in our hearts take time to mature and grow. My brother and cousin began to question in their hearts why I would make a decision that would lead to such seemingly terrible consequences as they were beating me. It was not until a later time that they came to me one night to ask me about it. I had no idea that my decision to accept the Lordship of Jesus Christ and obey Him would influence my two brothers' and several cousins' decisions to also follow Jesus and become fully committed to Him.

I did not know at that time that one of my cousins would become the pastor of the Adventist church in which I was baptized. I did not know that, thirty years later, my mom would become a fully devoted follower of Jesus and be baptized into the Adventist Church. When I accepted Jesus Christ, I had no idea I would be alive today. Thirty years after I was beaten and humiliated, I discovered that I am alive because of my obedience to God. If I had stayed in Iraq, I likely would have been killed as a result of one of the five wars Iraq has waged since then.

We want everything immediately. But the Lord says, "Be still, and know that I am God" (Psalm 46:10). God does not say to be quiet. He says to remain calm. Do not be uptight or afraid because He is in charge of your life. David, furthermore, encourages us that while we are waiting, we need to trust in the Lord. "Some trust in chariots and some in horses, but we trust in the name of the LORD our God" (Psalm 20:7).

The Lord urges us, "Wait upon and trust Me. I will take care of you." Trust and patience are intertwined in our experiences. We will not know some of God's leading until we reach heaven. One day soon, we will gather around a Messianic table; Jesus will be at the head of the table, and you and I will be sitting there. Jesus Himself will explain to us His leading in our lives and how He made all things to work for our good. I can hardly wait for that day!

As you are waiting, "make God your entire trust. Pray, pray, pray, pray in faith. Trust then the keeping of your soul to God. He will keep that which is committed to Him against that day. . . . Trust fully, unwaveringly in God."[4] Wait, watch, and pray.

---

1. White, *Steps to Christ*, 89.

2. White, *Steps to Christ*, 88.

3. Dictionary of Bible Themes, BibleGateway.com, s.v. "5,647 Promises, Divine," accessed March 7, 2017, https://www.biblegateway.com/resources/dictionary-of-bible-themes/5467-promises-divine.

4. Ellen G. White, *Reflecting Christ* (Hagerstown, MD: Review and Herald®, 2009), 120.

Reflection

God's Fullness Is Everything in My Life

*But one thing I do: Forgetting what is behind and straining
toward what is ahead, I press on toward the goal to win the prize
for which God has called me heavenward in Christ Jesus.*
—Philippians 3:13, 14

As I look back over my life, I see how God was always leading. There were four defining divine appointments.

The first major event was the providential walk that led me to the Adventist church to watch the movie about Jesus and fall in love with Him. The life, death, and resurrection of Jesus was so amazing. The movie thrilled my heart and put me on a lifelong pursuit to know Him.

When you really learn about Jesus, you will fall in love with Him too. The more you feel His love for you, the more you will want to do things to honor and glorify Him.

The second major event was responding positively to the Holy Spirit's prompting. As I heard the message on martyrdom and the importance of faithfulness to God at the Orthodox church, I decided to follow Jesus. I am so glad the Holy Spirit spoke to my heart through the ministry of the Orthodox priest and that I said yes to the Lord.

God speaks to us in many different ways. Maybe this book has spoken to you, maybe a sermon, maybe a song, or maybe a friend talking to you. I urge you to respond positively to the Holy Spirit's prompting.

The third major event was staying faithful to Jesus and not taking my exams on the Sabbath. It was very difficult to do that, but God empowered me. God will empower you to stay faithful. He will give you an extra measure of His grace to go through trials, temptations, and difficulties.

The fourth major event was meeting my cousin Suhelah ten years ago and finding out that God's faithfulness is the reason I am alive today. In addition, I did not know that when I decided to follow Jesus it would influence so many members of my family to do the same as well.

You might find yourself on the horns of a dilemma, but one day you will look back and see God's hand in everything.

I have followed Jesus for many years. My understanding of Him and His love has increased with time. The more I know Him, the more my appreciation and love for Him grows and the more I experience that He loves me and wants the best for me. More and more over the years, I have felt deeply that He is everything to me. He is my brother and my sister. He is my father and my mother. He is my best friend, the One I can go to and share all my problems and all my joys. The more I know Him, the more I feel He is my Lord and my Savior.

Is it worth it to follow Jesus? Is it worth it to go through the trouble? Yes, indeed!

Millions upon millions of people throughout the ages and all over the world add their testimony to mine and say, "Yes, indeed! It is worth it to follow Jesus." Will you follow Him today and be obedient to Him?

There might be someone reading this story who is struggling with the issues of faithfulness, such as keeping the Sabbath, Lordship, or commitment. I invite you today to break away, take your first step, and follow Jesus. He is worth it. He will take care of you.

My story demonstrates the amazing love of God and the importance of surrender to Him. It shows the incredible power of God released through prayer. This book testifies to the power of God in the life of one man from Nineveh. Just as God took care of me in many challenging circumstances, I know God will take care of you too. He will make all things to work for good for you.